The Mother Tongue
Student Workbook 2

George Lyman Kittredge
Sarah Louise Arnold

Adapted By
Amy M. Edwards and Christina J. Mugglin

BLUE SKY
DAISIES

The Mother Tongue Student Workbook 2
By Amy M. Edwards and Christina J. Mugglin © 2014

Exercises from *The Mother Tongue: Book II*
by George Lyman Kittredge, Sarah Louise Arnold © 1901, 1908

Published by Blue Sky Daisies
blueskydaisies.net

Cover design: © Blue Sky Daises 2021
ISBN-13: 978-0-9905529-2-5
ISBN-10: 0990552926

THE MOTHER TONGUE
Adapted for Modern Students
STUDENT WORKBOOK 2

The exercises in this book accompany the lessons in the text *The Mother Tongue, Adapted for Modern Students* by Amy M. Edwards and Christina J. Mugglin. The workbook exercises are presented in a format designed to make it easier for students to complete in their books. *Student Workbook 2* includes exercises for chapters 76-143.

Table of Contents

Chapter 76: Comparison of Adjectives, Part 1

There are no written exercises for chapter 76.

Chapter 77: Comparison of Adjectives, Part 2

I.

Write in three columns the following adjectives in the three degrees of comparison:

	POSITIVE	COMPARATIVE	SUPERLATIVE
1. bright			
2. lowly			
3. tall			
4. smooth			
5. rough			
6. quick			
7. nimble			
8. fierce			
9. black			
10. able			
11. subtle			
12. crazy			
13. mad			
14. sane			
15. muddy			
16. wet			

	POSITIVE	COMPARATIVE	SUPERLATIVE
17. dry			
18. red			
19. sad			
20. humble			

II.

Circle adjectives that are in the **comparative** or the **superlative degree**. **Write** the positive degree of each on the line. **Underline** the substantive to which each belongs.

1. He was a bigger boy than I.

   _____

2. They were some of the choicest troops of his whole army.

   _____

3. The town is one of the neatest in England.

   _____

4. Life is dearer than the golden ore.

   _____

5. Byron was, at his death, but a year younger than Burns.

   _____

6. On the highest part of the mountain is an old fortress.

   _____

7. The storm of passion insensibly subsided into calmer melancholy.

   _____

8. The sternest sum total of all worldly misfortunes is death.

   _____

9. Her astonishment now was greater than ever.

_____

10. The air grew colder and colder; the mist became thicker and thicker; the shrieks of the sea

fowl louder and louder.

_____

III.
Write three sentences for each adjective below. Use the positive degree, comparative degree, and superlative degree.

1. fast _____

_____

_____

2. pure _____

_____

_____

3. low _____

_____

_____

4. clumsy _____

_____

_____

5. high _____

_____

_____

6. large _____

_____

_____

7. brown _____

_____

_____

8. ragged _____

_____

_____

9. cross _____

_____

_____

10. deep _____

_____

_____

11. cheery _____

_____

_____

12. merry _____

_____

_____

13. short _____

_____

_____

14. hungry _____

_____

_____

15. quiet _____

_____

_____

16. green_____

_____

_____

17. manly _____

_____

_____

18. noble_____

_____

_____

19. severe _____

_____

_____

20. handsome _____

_____

_____

21. lovely _____

_____

_____

Chapter 78: Comparison of Adjectives, Part 3

Underline the adjectives in the comparative degree and **circle** adjectives in the superlative degree. Remember that the adverbs <u>more</u> and <u>most</u> are often used to change an adjective's degree.

1. The evening was more calm and lovely than any that yet had smiled upon our voyage.

2. The environs are most beautiful, and the village itself is one of the prettiest I ever saw.

3. Example is always more efficacious than precept.

4. The Edinburgh scholars of that period were more noted for clearness of head than for warmth of heart.

5. Nothing could be more bleak and saddening than the appearance of this lake.

6. The country became rougher, and the people more savage.

7. He sat down with a most gloomy countenance.

8. The Caliph remained in the most violent agitation.

9. A more extraordinary incident has seldom happened.

10. The wind was even more boisterous than usual.

11. The most elaborate preparations had been made.

12. The garret windows and housetops were so crowded with spectators that I thought in all my travels I had not seen a more populous place.

Chapter 79: Comparison of Adjectives, Part 4

Underline the comparatives and **circle** the superlatives.

1. He walked off without further ceremony.

2. A friend in the court is better than a penny in purse.

3. Caesar has been called the foremost man of all this world.

4. The inquisitive prince passed most of his nights on the summit of his tower.

5. I must confess your offer is the best.

6. The worst minds have often something of good principle in them.

7. So doth the greater glory dim the less.

8. This island was at a greater distance than I expected, and I did not reach it in less than five hours.

9. There are two or three more pens in the box.

10. I ne'er had worse luck in my life!

11. Lead the way without any more talking.

12. He grows worse and worse.

13. I said an elder soldier, not a better.

14. Orlando approached the man and found it was his brother, his elder brother.

15. Present fears are less than horrible imaginings.

16. That is Antonio, the duke's eldest son.

17. A sad tale's best for winter.

18. To fear the worst oft cures the worse.

19. The bird is perched on the topmost bough.

20. My title's good, and better far than his.

21. I have three daughters; the eldest is eleven.

22. To weep is to make less the depth of grief.

23. He has his health, and ampler strength, indeed,

    Than most have of his age.

24. I will use my utmost skill in his recovery.

25. Brutus' love to Caesar was no less than his.

26. My utmost efforts were fruitless.

27. We cannot defend the outer fortifications.

Chapter 80: Comparison of Adjectives, Part 5

There are no written exercises for chapter 80.

Chapter 81: Comparison of Adverbs

There are no written exercises for chapter 81.

Chapter 82: Irregular Comparison of Adverbs

In the following sentences **label** all the adverbs with **Adv** and **underline** the word that each modifies. If the adverb is capable of comparison, write its **three degrees on the line**. If its meaning makes it incapable of comparison, state that fact and give your reasons.

1. Youth seldom thinks of dangers.

    _____

2. To every man upon this earth

    Death cometh soon or late.

    _____

3. So the days passed peacefully away.

    _____

4. It would ill become me to boast of anything.

    _____

5. Delvile eagerly called to the coachman to drive up to the house, and anxiously begged

    Cecilia to sit still.

    _____

6. They came again and again, and were every time more welcome than before.

    _____

7. Perhaps this awkwardness will wear off hereafter.

    _____

8. And he, God wot, was forced to stand

    Oft for his right with blade in hand.

    _____

9. He heard a laugh full musical aloft.

    _____

10. The following morning Gertrude arose early.

    _____

11. She walks too fast, and speaks too fast.

_____

12. The seamen spied a rock within half a cable's length of the ship, but the wind was so strong
    that we were driven directly upon it, and immediately split.

_____

_____

13. Was that the king that spurred his horse so hard?

_____

14. "We know each other well."

    "We do, and long to know each other worse."

_____

15. He came too late; the ship was under sail.

_____

16. How slow this old moon wanes!

_____

17. Your judgment is absolutely correct.

_____

18. The tide rose higher and higher.

_____

19. He swims energetically but slowly.

_____

20. The courtiers were all most magnificently clad.

_____

Chapter 83: Use of Comparative and Superlative

I.

Make sentences in which you use the following adjectives and adverbs correctly.

better _____

_____

best _____

_____

sooner_____

_____

most agreeable _____

_____

nimbler_____

_____

nimblest_____

_____

most _____

_____

more _____

_____

quicker _____

_____

quickest _____

_____

smallest _____

_____

smaller _____

_____

most interesting _____

_____

slower_____

_____

slowest _____

_____

more accurate _____

_____

most accurate _____

_____

II.
Analyze the sentences that you have made in Exercise I.
   (1) **Underline** complete subject **once** and complete predicate **twice**.
   (2) **Label** simple subject with **S** and simple predicate with **V**.
   (3) **Place** parentheses around phrases and brackets around clauses.
   (4) **Label** any predicate adjectives with **PA** and predicate nominatives with **PN**.
   (5) **Label** any direct objects with **DO** and indirect objects with **IO**.
   (6) **Label** modifiers (adverbs with **Adv**, adjectives with **Adj**, adverb clauses with **Adv**, and adjective clauses with **Adj**).

III.
Fill in the blanks with adjectives or adverbs in the comparative or the superlative degree as the meaning requires. You will need to **write** the italicized word's ending (e.g. -r or -st) or choose the correct italicized word given in parentheses and **write** it in the blank.

Be prepared to explain to your teacher the grounds of your choice in each case.

1. Tom and I are friends. Indeed he is the (*better* or *best*) _____ friend I have.

2. Which is the (*more* or *most*) _____ studious of your two sisters?

3. Both generals are brave, but the *old*_____ is of course the (*more* or *most*) _____ experienced of the two.

4. Of all the men in our company I think the very *brave*_____ was Corporal Jackson.

5. Texas is the *large*_____ of the United States.

6. Which is *large*_____, Chicago or Philadelphia?

7. Mention the *large*_____ city in the world.

8. I don't know which I like (*better* or *best*) _____, history or arithmetic.

9. Which do you like (*better* or *best*) _____, history, arithmetic, or reading?

10. I like history (*better* or *best*)_____ than anything else.

11. Of all my studies I like history (*better* or *best*) _____.

12. Which is the *heavi*_____, a pound of feathers or a pound of gold?

13. Which is the *heavi*_____, a pound of feathers, a pound of lead, or a pound of gold?

14. Jane is the *tall*_____ of the family.

IV.
Compare the following adverbs by writing the **comparative** and **superlative degree**.

1. soon _____

2. often _____

3. badly_____

4. well_____

5. noisily_____

6. merrily _____

7. far _____

8. much_____

9. furiously _____

V.
Use the **superlative** of each adverb in Exercise IV above in a sentence of your own.

1. soon _____

2. often _____

3. badly_____

4. well_____

5. noisily_____

6. merrily _____

7. far _____

8. much_____

9. furiously _____

Chapter 84: Demonstrative Pronouns and Adjectives

Write twenty sentences, each containing a demonstrative (*this*, *that*, *these*, or *those*). Examine each sentence, and **write** whether you have used the demonstrative as a substantive pronoun (subject or object) or as a limiting adjective (adjectively).

FOR EXAMPLE: *This* is a tasty strawberry. **Substantive pronoun**
Those cars are for sale. **Limiting adjective**

1. _____

_____

2. _____

_____

3. _____

_____

4. _____

_____

5. _____

_____

6. _____

_____

7. _____

_____

8. _____

_____

9. _____

_____

10. _____

_____

11. _____

_____

12. _____

_____

13. _____

_____

14. _____

_____

15. _____

_____

16. _____

_____

17. _____

_____

18. _____

_____

19. _____

_____

20. _____

_____

Chapter 85: Inflection of Demonstratives

I.

Underline each demonstrative in the sentences below. Fill in the chart, identifying if each demonstrative is a pronoun or adjective and singular or plural. If it is a pronoun, give its case.

	PRONOUN (PRO) OR ADJECTIVE (ADJ)?	NUMBER (S/P)	NOMINATIVE (N), OBJECTIVE (O), OR GENITIVE (G) CASE?
1. This is the whole truth.			
2. This apple is sour.			
3. These men are brave.			
4. That is a strange fish.			
5. That story is false.			
6. Are you sure of that?			
7. John told me this.			
8. These are facts.			

II.

Underline the demonstratives below. **Label** those used substantively (as a subject or object) with **S** and those used adjectively (as a limiting adjective) with **Adj**.

1. These thoughts did not hinder him from sleeping soundly.

2. These are Clan-Alpine's warriors true.

3. Loth as they were, these gentlemen had nothing for it but to obey.

4. "Major Buckley," I said, "What horse is that?"

5. Nor yet for this, even as a spy,

   Hadst thou, unheard, been doomed to die.

6. Ill with King James's mood that day

   Suited gay feast and minstrel lay.

7. That horse's history would be worth writing.

8. All this was meant to be as irritating as possible.

9. These fertile plains, that softened vale,

   Were once the birthright of the Gael.

10. Many hundred large volumes have been published upon this controversy.

11. What a good old man that is!

12. That absolves me from any responsibility.

13. Jim will be sorry to hear of this.

14. To hear this beautiful voice after so long a silence — to find those calm, dark, friendly eyes

    regarding him — bewildered him, or gave him courage, he knew not which.

15. This murderous chief, this ruthless man,

    This head of a rebellious clan,

    Hath led thee safe, through watch and ward,

    Far past Clan-Alpine's outmost guard.

16. Those are terrible questions.

17. These were the strong points in his favor.

18. I'll fill these dogged spies with false reports.

19. These soldiers are Danes, those are Swedes.

20. Can you hesitate long between this and that?

Chapter 86: Indefinite Pronouns and Adjectives

Parse the indefinite pronouns, nouns, and adjectives by writing each word on the line provided, identify it, and tell what part of speech it is in the sentence. The first one is done for you.

Indefinite pronouns/adjectives: *each, every, either, both, neither, some, any, such, none, other, another, each other, one another.*

Indefinite nouns: *everybody, everything, anybody, anything*

1. They talked about each other's books for hours.

   each other's: indefinite compound pronoun, genitive adjective modifying books

2. Some war, some plague, some famine they foresee.

   _____

3. The two armies encountered one another at Towton Field, near Tadcaster. No such battle had been seen in England since the fight of Senlac.

   _____

   _____

4. The morning was raw, and a dense fog was over everything.

   _____

5. Some wild young colts were let out of the stockyard.

   _____

6. They tell one another all they know, and often more too.

   _____

7. Bate me some and I will pay you some.

   _____

8. I do not wish any companion in the world but you.

   _____

9. The big round tears coursed one another down his innocent nose.

_____

10. Grace and remembrance be to you both.

_____

11. I know it pleaseth neither of us well.

_____

12. Each hurries toward his home.

_____

13. Gentlemen both, you will mistake each other.

_____

_____

14. No such apology is necessary.

_____

15. Does either of you care for this?

_____

16. Mine honor is my life. Both grow in one.

_____

_____

17. The parcels contained some letters and verses.

_____

18. Think you there was ever such a man?

_____

19. A black day will it be to somebody.

_____

20. Friend, we understand not one another.

_____

Chapter 87: The Self-Pronouns

In the following sentences **underline** all the self-pronouns. In the blank provided **write** whether it is an **intensive pronoun** or a **reflexive pronoun.**

If it is an intensive pronoun, **draw an arrow** to the noun or pronoun with which it is in apposition. If it is reflexive, **draw an arrow** back to the verb or preposition of which it is the object and **circle** the noun or pronoun to which each refers back.

Remember to ask:

Is it emphasizing a substantive? It is an intensive pronoun.

Is it the object of a transitive verb or preposition? It is a reflexive pronoun.

1. The people abandoned themselves to despair. _____

2. Jack sat by himself in a corner. _____

3. They have talked themselves hoarse. _____

4. The men themselves carried no provisions except a bag of oatmeal. _____

5. Envy shoots at others, and wounds herself._____

6. We ourselves were wrapped up in our furs. _____

7. Clifford wrapped himself in an old cloak. _____

8. I myself am to blame for this._____

9. I shall hardly know myself in a blue dress. _____

10. I have not words to express the poor man's thankfulness, neither could he express it

    himself. _____

11. Every guilty deed holds in itself the seed of retribution._____

12. Jane herself opened the door. _____

13. She amused herself with walking and reading. _____

14. The story itself was scarcely credible. _____

15. The lieutenant was presented to Washington himself._____

16. Nobody save myself so much as turned to look after him. _____

17. One seldom dislikes one's self._____

18. The guides themselves had lost the path._____

19. The prisoner threw himself into the sea and swam for the shore. _____

20. The old clock itself looked weary. _____

21. Guard thyself from false friends. _____

22. You must prepare yourself for the worst._____

23. You cannot protect yourselves from wrong. _____

Chapter 88: Special Uses of the Self-Pronouns

There are no written exercises for this chapter.

Chapter 89: Numerals

Underline each numeral and **write** in the blank provided whether it is an adjective (cardinal, ordinal, or other), a noun, or an adverb.

1. Twice through the hall the chieftain strode._____

2. Hundreds in this little town are upon the point of starving._____

3. I have paid you fourfold. _____

4. The third time never fails._____

5. The English lie within fifteen hundred paces of your tents. _____

6. Methought I saw a thousand fearful wrecks._____

7. The threefold shield protected him. _____

8. They shouted thrice; what was the last cry for? _____

9. Yet thousands still desire to journey on._____

10. Byron died in the thirty-seventh year of his age. _____

11. This note doth tell me of ten thousand French _____

   That in the field lie slain: of princes, in this number,

   And nobles bearing banners, there lie dead

   One hundred twenty-six: added to these, _____

   Of knights, esquires, and gallant gentlemen,

   Eight thousand and four hundred. _____

Chapter 89: Review Exercise[1]

In the space provided, analyze these sentences and parse the substantives. The first one is done for you.

To analyze the sentences:
  (1) **Underline** complete subject **once** and complete predicate **twice**.
  (2) **Label** simple subject with **S** and simple predicate with **V**.
  (3) **Place** brackets around clauses and parentheses around phrases. **Label** the parts of prepositional phrases with **P** for the preposition and **OP** for the object.
  (4) **Label** any predicate adjectives **Pred Adj** and predicate nominatives **PN**.
  (5) **Label** any direct objects **DO**, indirect objects **IO** and conjunctions with **C**.
  (6) **Label** modifiers (adverbs **Adv**, adjectives **Adj**, adverb clauses **Adv**, and adjective clauses **Adj**).

To **parse** the substantives, write the following information about each one:
  1. case (N, O, G)
  2. gender (M, F, N)
  3. number (S, P)

```
   V    S    V    DO   (Adv)   Adv
```
1. Will you shake hands (with me) now? _____

_____ you: N, M/F, S _____ hands: O, N, P _____

2. Delay not, Caesar!   Read it instantly! _____

_____

3. Lay thy finger on thy lips._____

_____

----

[1] Here the inflection of nouns, pronouns, adjectives, and adverbs (chapters 61-89) should be reviewed. Sections 237-242 will serve as a summary, and should accordingly be studied at this point. The miscellaneous sentences on this page give examples of various forms and constructions and may be used for practice in parsing and analysis at the close of the review.

Note: Sentence 25 appears as sentence 3 in the *Mother Tongue: Adapted for Modern Students*

4. Have you ever had your house burnt down? _____

_____

5. Did you take me for Roger Bacon? _____

_____

6. What, has this thing appeared again tonight? _____

_____

7. Our neighbor's big black mastiff sprang over the fence. _____

_____

_____

8. Theodore's cousin has just returned from Asia. _____

_____

_____

9. The jay's noisy chatter silenced our talk. _____

_____

_____

10. The old pilot's skill saved the ship from destruction. _____

_____

_____

11. I owe you much already. _____

_____

12. They shall fetch thee jewels from the deep. _____

_____

_____

13. I sell thee poison; thou hast sold me none. _____

_____

_____

14. Sing high the praise of Denmark's host. _____

_____

15. Pen never told his mother a falsehood. _____

_____

_____

16. Last night the very gods showed me a vision._____

_____

17. He strode down the creaking stair. _____

_____

18. The ruling passion conquers reason still. _____

_____

19. Four seasons fill the measure of the year._____

_____

20. He feels the anxieties of life. _____

_____

_____

21. The long carpets rose along the gusty floor._____

_____

22. The needle plies its busy task. _____

_____

23. I spent some time in Holland. _____

_____

24. Great offices will have great talents. _____

_____

25. Do you not know that every hard, cold word you use is one stone on a great pyramid of

useless remorse? _____

_____

_____

Chapter 90: Inflection of Verbs — Tense

There are no written exercises for chapter 90.

Chapter 91: Preterite (Past) Tense

In each sentence **change** the **present tense to preterite (past tense)**. Tell whether each past tense verb (preterite) that you have made is **weak** or **strong**.

1. I ride to Hyde Park. _____

_____

2. The country becomes disturbed, and nightly meetings of the peasantry take place.

_____

_____

3. Many of the boldest sink beneath the fear of betrayal._____

_____

4. When Calabressa calls at the house in Curzon Street he is at once admitted. _____

_____

5. He walks on, his heart full of an audacious joy. _____

_____

6. Returning to the cottage, he proceeds to sweep the hearth and make up the fire.

_____

_____

(Chapter 91 exercise continued on next page.)

7. Where the remote Bermudas ride

   In the Ocean's bosom unespied,

   From a small boat that rows along,

   The listening winds receive this song.

   _____

   _____

   _____

   _____

8. Many fresh streams run to one salt sea. _____

   _____

9. The camels from their keepers break;

   The distant steer forsakes the yoke._____

   _____

10. Lady Evelyn is a tall, somewhat good-looking, elderly lady, who wears her silver-white

    hair in old-fashioned curls._____

    _____

    _____

11. His faded yellow hair begins to grow thin, and his thread-bare frock coat hangs limp from

    sloping shoulders. _____

    _____

    _____

12. I wander lonely as a cloud._____

    _____

13. The next morning he comes down to the breakfast room earlier than is his custom, and

salutes everybody there with great cordiality. _____

_____

_____

14. To the belfry, one by one, haste the ringers. _____

_____

15. No haughty feat of arms I tell. _____

_____

16. The senators mean to establish Caesar as a king. _____

_____

17. I rest two or three minutes, and then give the boat another shove, and so on, till the sea

is no higher than my armpits. _____

_____

_____

18. His heart jumps with pleasure as the famous university comes in view. _____

_____

_____

Chapter 92: Preterite (Past) Tense of Strong (Irregular) Verbs

There are no written exercises for this chapter.

Chapter 93: Weak Preterites (Regular Past Tense) in *-ed* or *-d*

Make sentences containing the **preterites (past tense)** of the following weak verbs:

1. act _____

_____

2. govern _____

_____

3. rush _____

_____

4. knock _____

_____

5. fish _____

_____

6. tend _____

_____

7. tell _____

_____

8. rattle _____

_____

9. carry _____

_____

10. delay _____

_____

11. flee _____

_____

12. try _____

_____

13. address _____

_____

14. pitch _____

_____

15. talk _____

_____

16. experiment _____

_____

17. describe _____

_____

18. rebel _____

_____

Chapter 94: Weak Preterites (Past Tense) in -*t*

There are no written exercises for chapter 94.

Chapter 95: Weak Preterites Without Ending

I.
Make sentences containing the **preterite (past tense)** of the following verbs, some of which are weak and some strong. If you need help check the list of verbs in Appendix B of your text, or check a dictionary.

1. bend _____

2. sell _____

3. act _____

4. review _____

5. try _____

6. spin _____

7. drink _____

8. eat _____

9. carry _____

10. lose _____

11. compel _____

12. read _____

13. lead _____

14. tread _____

15. leave _____

16. work _____

17. spend _____

18. know _____

19. set _____

20. sit _____

21. lie _____

22. lay _____

23. rend_____

24. bring_____

25. rear _____

26. arise _____

27. ring_____

28. break _____

29. bind _____

30. copy _____

31. spare_____

32. multiply _____

33. catch _____

34. divide_____

35. subtract _____

36. telegraph _____

37. strike_____

38. run _____

39. wrestle _____

40. blow _____

41. burst _____

42. climb_____

43. sing _____

44. begin_____

45. stand_____

46. understand _____

47. go _____

48. change _____

49. teach _____

50. reach _____

51. split_____

II.

Double underline all the preterites (past tense verbs), and **mark** above the verb whether they are weak with **W** or strong with **S**. Also **write** the present tense in each case.

When midnight drew near, and when the robbers from afar saw that no light was

burning and that everything appeared quiet, their captain said to them that he thought that

they had run away without reason, telling one of them to go and reconnoitre. So one of them

went, and found everything quite quiet. He went into the kitchen to strike a light, and, taking

the glowing fiery-eyes of the cat for burning coals, he held a match to them in order to kindle

it. But the cat, not seeing the joke, flew into his face, spitting and scratching.

III.

Fill each blank with a **preterite** (past tense verbs). Mark whether each preterite is weak with **W** or strong with **S**.

1. The hunter took careful aim and _____; but the deer _____ away

   unharmed.

2. A portrait of Mr. Gilbert _____ on the wall.

3. I _____ my companion to lend me his knife.

4. In the distance _____ the lights of the village.

5. The sailor _____ into the sea and _____ to the rescue.

6. The boy _____ on the burning deck.

7. The kite _____ majestically into the air.

8. A puff of wind _____ off the boy's cap and it _____ along the ground. He

   _____ after it as fast as he could. The faster he _____, the faster the cap

   _____.

9. The mischievous fellow _____ three leaves out of my book.

10. The maid _____ the bucket with water and _____ it to the thirsty wayfarers.

11. Tom _____ on a rock, fishing patiently.

12. The miser _____ a hole to conceal his treasure.

13. Joe _____ the tree to get some apples.

Chapter 96: Singular and Plural Verbs

I.

Fill in the blanks with a singular or a plural verb in the present tense.
Mark above the verb with **S** if singular and with **P** if plural in number.

1. I _____ sorry to hear of your misfortune.

2. We _____ ball every Saturday afternoon.

3. He _____ the strongest swimmer in the school.

4. They _____ very good friends of mine.

5. It _____ a great deal of money to build a railroad.

6. John and Tom always _____ to school together.

7. Birds _____; fishes _____; snakes _____; dogs _____ on four

   legs; mankind alone _____ upright.

8. You _____ so badly that I can hardly read your letter. Your brother _____ much

   better.

9. The farmer _____ the seed; but the sun and the rain _____ it grow.

10. My uncle _____ me a dollar whenever he _____ to visit us.

11. Kangaroos _____ very long hind legs.

12. A spider _____ eight legs; a beetle _____ six.

13. My pony _____ apples out of my hand.

14. The grocer _____ tea, sugar, salt, and molasses.

15. The company of soldiers _____ up the hill in the face of the enemy.

16. The grapes _____ in clusters on the vine.

II.

Using the sentences from the chapter 79 exercise, reproduced below, identify the following:

1. **Underline** the subjects, **double underline** verbs and verb phrases.
2. **Circle** the objects, (direct objects, indirect objects, objects of the preposition)
3. **Label** the number of the subject (**S/P**) and the verb (**S/P**).

Remember that sometimes the subject of the sentence is a phrase or clause.

1. He walked off without further ceremony.

2. A friend in the court is better than a penny in purse.

3. Caesar has been called the foremost man of all this world.

4. The inquisitive prince passed most of his nights on the summit of his tower.

5. I must confess your offer is the best.

6. The worst minds have often something of good principle in them.

7. So doth the greater glory dim the less.

8. This island was at a greater distance than I expected, and I did not reach it in less than five hours.

9. There are two or three more pens in the box.[2]

10. I ne'er had worse luck in my life!

11. Lead the way without any more talking.

12. He grows worse and worse.

13. I said an elder soldier, not a better.

14. Orlando approached the man and found it was his brother, his elder brother.

15. Present fears are less than horrible imaginings.

---

[2] Be careful! *There* is not the subject in this sentence.

16. That is Antonio, the duke's eldest son.

17. A sad tale's best for winter.

18. To fear the worst oft cures the worse.

19. The bird is perched on the topmost bough.

20. My title's good, and better far than his.

21. I have three daughters; the eldest is eleven.

22. To weep is to make less the depth of grief.

23. He has his health, and ampler strength, indeed,

    Than most have of his age.

24. I will use my utmost skill in his recovery.

25. Brutus' love to Caesar was no less than his.

26. My utmost efforts were fruitless.

27. We cannot defend the outer fortifications.

III.
Using the sentences from the chapter 85, Exercise II, reproduced below, identify the following:
1. **Underline** the subjects, **double underline** verbs and verb phrases.
2. **Circle** the objects, (direct objects, indirect objects, objects of the preposition)
3. **Label** the number of the subject (**S/P**) and the verb (**S/P**).

1. These thoughts did not hinder him from sleeping soundly.

2. These are Clan-Alpine's warriors true.

3. Loth as they were, these gentlemen had nothing for it but to obey.

4. "Major Buckley," I said, "What horse is that?"

5. Nor yet for this, even as a spy,

    Hadst thou, unheard, been doomed to die.

6. Ill with King James's mood that day

    Suited gay feast and minstrel lay.

7. That horse's history would be worth writing.

8. All this was meant to be as irritating as possible.

9. These fertile plains, that softened vale,

    Were once the birthright of the Gael.

10. Many hundred large volumes have been published upon this controversy.

11. What a good old man that is!

12. That absolves me from any responsibility.

13. Jim will be sorry to hear of this.

14. To hear this beautiful voice after so long a silence — to find those calm, dark, friendly eyes

    regarding him — bewildered him, or gave him courage, he knew not which.

15. This murderous chief, this ruthless man,

    This head of a rebellious clan,

    Hath led thee safe, through watch and ward,

    Far past Clan-Alpine's outmost guard.

16. Those are terrible questions.

17. These were the strong points in his favor.

18. I'll fill these dogged spies with false reports.

19. These soldiers are Danes, those are Swedes.

20. Can you hesitate long between this and that?

Chapter 97: Special Rules for the Number of Verbs

There are no written exercises for chapter 97.

Chapter 98: Person of Verbs

I.

In the space below, write an account of some accident or adventure that you have had or that you have heard of.

_____

_____

_____

_____

_____

_____

_____

_____

_____

_____

If you have written in the first person, change your story so that it shall be told of some other person. If you have told your story in the third person, imagine that the adventure happened to you, and write the story again in the first person.

_____

_____

_____

_____

_____

_____

_____

_____

_____

_____

_____

What changes have you made in the form of each verb?

_____

_____

II.

Find some story in your history or reading book, or you may use the selection printed below, which is taken from H. E. Marshall's *Our Island Story*. Imagine that the incidents related happened to you, and tell the story in the first person.

> When Prince Hal came to the throne in 1413 A.D., he gave up all his wild ways and tried to rule as a wise king should. Judge Gascoigne was much afraid that he would suffer now for having sent the Prince to prison. But Henry had a noble mind. He knew that the judge had only done what was right. So after he became king, Henry treated Judge Gascoigne as a friend, and when he gave up his judgeship it was because he was a very old man. "Still be my judge," he said, "and if I should ever have a son who does wrong, I hope you will punish him as you did me."

_____

_____

_____

_____

_____

_____

_____

_____

_____

_____

_____

_____

_____

_____

_____

_____

_____

_____

_____

_____

What changes have you made in the form of each verb?

_____

_____

III.

Circle the person and number of each of the verbs and verb phrases below. If the form may belong to more than one person or number, circle each one. Test your accuracy by using personal pronouns (*I, you, they,* etc.) with each form. Some of the verb forms use the archaic second person singular form, which is used with *thou*. For example, *Thou didst know.*

If you are unsure about a verb, check Appendix B.

	SINGULAR			PLURAL		
1. found	1st	2nd	3rd	1st	2nd	3rd
2. didst know	1st	2nd	3rd	1st	2nd	3rd
3. finds	1st	2nd	3rd	1st	2nd	3rd
4. acts	1st	2nd	3rd	1st	2nd	3rd
5. act	1st	2nd	3rd	1st	2nd	3rd
6. mentions	1st	2nd	3rd	1st	2nd	3rd
7. sells	1st	2nd	3rd	1st	2nd	3rd
8. sold	1st	2nd	3rd	1st	2nd	3rd
9. broughtest	1st	2nd	3rd	1st	2nd	3rd
10. brings	1st	2nd	3rd	1st	2nd	3rd
11. bringest	1st	2nd	3rd	1st	2nd	3rd
12. speak	1st	2nd	3rd	1st	2nd	3rd
13. spoke	1st	2nd	3rd	1st	2nd	3rd
14. broke	1st	2nd	3rd	1st	2nd	3rd
15. endeavors	1st	2nd	3rd	1st	2nd	3rd
16. dives	1st	2nd	3rd	1st	2nd	3rd
17. replied	1st	2nd	3rd	1st	2nd	3rd
18. puzzled	1st	2nd	3rd	1st	2nd	3rd
19. utters	1st	2nd	3rd	1st	2nd	3rd
20. knowest	1st	2nd	3rd	1st	2nd	3rd
21. hath	1st	2nd	3rd	1st	2nd	3rd
22. has	1st	2nd	3rd	1st	2nd	3rd
23. canst	1st	2nd	3rd	1st	2nd	3rd
24. can	1st	2nd	3rd	1st	2nd	3rd

	SINGULAR			PLURAL		
25. is	1st	2nd	3rd	1st	2nd	3rd
26. are	1st	2nd	3rd	1st	2nd	3rd
27. leapest	1st	2nd	3rd	1st	2nd	3rd
28. fight	1st	2nd	3rd	1st	2nd	3rd
29. fought	1st	2nd	3rd	1st	2nd	3rd
30. has spoken	1st	2nd	3rd	1st	2nd	3rd
31. have	1st	2nd	3rd	1st	2nd	3rd
32. am	1st	2nd	3rd	1st	2nd	3rd
33. art	1st	2nd	3rd	1st	2nd	3rd
34. were	1st	2nd	3rd	1st	2nd	3rd

IV.

In some page of your reading book, or in the following selection from Lewis Carroll's *Through the Looking-Glass*, **underline** all the **present tense** and **preterite tense verbs** you can. Tell the person and number of each. The first sentence is done for you below. (Don't worry about future tense or other verb forms, such as participles and infinitives, as you have not studied them yet.)

Alice <u>looked</u> on with great interest as the King <u>took</u> an enormous memorandum-book out of his pocket, and <u>began</u> writing. A sudden thought struck her, and she took hold of the end of the pencil, which came some way over his shoulder, and began writing for him.

The poor King looked puzzled and unhappy, and struggled with the pencil for some time without saying anything; but Alice was too strong for him, and at last he panted out "My dear! I really *must* get a thinner pencil. I can't manage this one a bit. It writes all manner of things that I don't intend--"

"What manner of things?" said the Queen, looking over the book (in which Alice had put *'The White Knight is sliding down the poker. He balances very badly'*) "That's not a memorandum of *your* feelings!"

There was a book lying near Alice on the table, and while she sat watching the White King (for she was still a little anxious about him, and had the ink all ready to throw over him, in case he fainted again), she turned over the leaves, to find some part that she could read, "---for it's all in some language I don't know," she said to herself.

looked: third person, singular, preterite (past) _____

took: third person, singular, preterite (past) _____

began: third person, singular, preterite (past) _____

_____

_____

_____

_____

_____

Chapter 99: Personal Endings — Conjugating Verbs

I.

In accordance with the model given in the text, conjugate the following verbs in the **present** and the **preterite** (past) tense. The first one is done for you. (Your teacher may allow you to conjugate the second person singular "Thou lovest," with the plural form, "You love," since this is the modern convention.)

VERB	PRESENT TENSE		PRETERITE (PAST) TENSE	
	SINGULAR	PLURAL	SINGULAR	PLURAL
love	*love* *lovest* *loves*	*love* *love* *love*	*loved* *lovedst* *loved*	*loved* *loved* *loved*
call				
answer				
shout				
examine				
stand				
find				
bind				

VERB	PRESENT TENSE		PRETERITE (PAST) TENSE	
	SINGULAR	PLURAL	SINGULAR	PLURAL
bear				
lose				
sit				
set				
lie (to tell a falsehood)				
lay				
burn				
fight				
bring				
catch				

VERB	PRESENT TENSE		PRETERITE (PAST) TENSE	
	SINGULAR	PLURAL	SINGULAR	PLURAL
reach				
spend				
beat				
declare				
read				
march				
charge				
enlarge				
despise				
praise				

VERB	PRESENT TENSE		PRETERITE (PAST) TENSE	
	SINGULAR	PLURAL	SINGULAR	PLURAL
honor				
foretell				
prophesy				
enter				
depart				

II.

Write the verbs in the blank provided and **circle** the number (**S/P**) and person (**1/2/3**) of each verb. Sentences from chapter 69, Exercise I, reproduced below.

1. He was my friend, faithful and just to me.

   _____ S P 1 2 3

2. Mahomet accompanied his uncle on trading journeys.

   _____ S P 1 2 3

3. Our Clifford was a happy youth.

   _____ S P 1 2 3

4. And now, child, what art thou doing?

   _____ S P 1 2 3

5. I think I can guess what you mean.

   _____ S P 1 2 3

   _____ S P 1 2 3

   _____ S P 1 2 3

6. Then boast no more your mighty deeds!

   _____ S P 1 2 3

7. Round him night resistless closes fast.

   _____ S P 1 2 3

8. I was in the utmost astonishment, and roared so loud that they all ran back in fright.

   _____ S P 1 2 3

   _____ S P 1 2 3

   _____ S P 1 2 3

9. She listens, but she cannot hear

The foot of horse, the voice of man.

_____   S   P   1   2   3

_____   S   P   1   2   3

10. He hollowed a boat of the birchen bark,

_____   S   P   1   2   3

Which carried him off from shore.

_____   S   P   1   2   3

11. At dead of night their sails were filled.

_____   S   P   1   2   3

12. Men at some time are masters of their fates.

_____   S   P   1   2   3

13. Here is a sick man that would speak with you.

_____   S   P   1   2   3

_____   S   P   1   2   3

14. Why should we yet our sail unfurl?

_____   S   P   1   2   3

15. I once more thought of attempting to break my bonds.

_____   S   P   1   2   3

16. Our fortune and fame had departed.

_____   S   P   1   2   3

17. The Hawbucks came in their family coach, with the blood-red hand emblazoned all over it.

_____ S P   1 2 3

_____ S P   1 2 3

18. The spoken word cannot be recalled. It must go on its way for good or evil.

_____ S P   1 2 3

_____ S P   1 2 3

19. He saw the lake, and a meteor bright

_____ S P   1 2 3

Quick over its surface played.

_____ S P   1 2 3

20. I have endeavored to solve this difficulty another way.

_____ S P   1 2 3

21. The military part of his life has furnished him with many adventures.

_____ S P   1 2 3

22. He ambled alongside the footpath on which they were walking, showing his discomfort by

a twist of his neck every few seconds.

_____ S P   1 2 3

_____ S P   1 2 3

23. Our provisions held out well, our ship was stanch, and our crew all in good health; but we

lay in the utmost distress for water.

_____ S P   1 2 3

_____ S P   1 2 3

_____ S P   1 2 3

24. Sweet day, so cool, so calm, so bright—

    The bridal of the earth and sky—

    The dew shall weep thy fall tonight,

    For thou must die.

    _____ S   P   1 2 3

    _____ S   P   1 2 3

25. Lend me thy cloak, Sir Thomas.

    _____ S   P   1 2 3

26. Captain Fluellen, you must come presently to the mines. The Duke of Gloucester would

    speak with you.

    _____ S   P   1 2 3

    _____ S   P   1 2 3

27. Madam, what should we do?

    _____ S   P   1 2 3

28. Worthy Macbeth, we stay upon your leisure.

    _____ S   P   1 2 3

29. Fair and noble hostess,

    We are your guest tonight.

    _____ S   P   1 2 3

III.

Conjugate the following verbs in the present tense, giving all three persons and both numbers. Use a pronoun as the subject of each verb.

VERB	PRESENT TENSE	
	SINGULAR	PLURAL
love	*I love.* *Thou lovest.* *He loves.*	*We love.* *You love.* *They love.*
stand		
answer		
compel		
go		
ask		
fill		
try		
succeed		

Verb	Present Tense	
	Singular	Plural
spend		
earn		
study		
run		
rescue		
play		
climb		
flee		
retreat		
charge		

VERB	PRESENT TENSE	
	SINGULAR	PLURAL
descend		
ride		
act		
smile		
laugh		
speed		
descry		
find		
bring		
discover		

Verb	Present Tense	
	Singular	Plural
desire		
retreat		
succeed		
drink		
lead		
bend		

IV.

For each instruction below, choose a different verb from Exercise III and form a sentence with that verb in the tense, person, and number given.

PRESENT TENSE

1. third person singular _____

_____

2. third person plural _____

_____

3. third person plural _____

_____

4. second person plural _____

_____

5. first person plural _____

_____

6. first person plural _____

_____

PRETERITE TENSE

7. first person singular _____

_____

8. first person singular _____

_____

9. third person plural _____

_____

10. second person plural _____

_____

11. second person plural _____

_____

12. third person singular _____

_____

13. third person singular _____

_____

Chapter 100: Infinitive

I.

Make sentences of your own containing the following infinitives:

1. to boast _____

_____

2. to help _____

_____

3. to leap _____

_____

4. to fly _____

_____

5. to flee _____

_____

6. to lie _____

_____

7. to lay _____

_____

8. to ask _____

_____

9. to advise _____

_____

10. to assist _____

_____

11. to order _____

_____

12. to revenge _____

_____

13. to describe _____

_____

14. to injure _____

_____

15. to disappear _____

_____

16. to lose _____

_____

17. to advance _____

_____

18. to recognize _____

_____

19. to travel _____

_____

20. to transform _____

_____

21. to spare _____

_____

22. to suggest _____

_____

23. to pursue _____

_____

24. to remember _____

_____

25. to remind _____

_____

26. to define _____

_____

27. to desert _____

_____

28. to settle _____

_____

29. to build _____

_____

30. to plant _____

_____

31. to exterminate _____

_____

32. to destroy _____

_____

33. to cultivate _____

_____

34. to sow _____

_____

35. to reap _____

_____

36. to mow _____

_____

37. to pacify _____

_____

38. to burn _____

_____

39. to descend _____

_____

40. to modify _____

_____

41. to persevere _____

_____

42. to forgive _____

_____

43. to puzzle _____

_____

44. to explain _____

_____

II.

Insert an infinitive with *to* in each blank.

EXAMPLE:

Tom is too tired__*to study*____ his lesson.

1. Old Carlo was too well trained _____ cats.

2. Charles was in such a hurry that he could hardly spare time _____ his breakfast.

3. We are taught _____ our enemies.

4. Gerald rose very early and went down to the brook _____ for trout.

5. Little Bo-Peep has lost her sheep,

   And doesn't know where _____ them.

6. The fireman was obliged _____ from the locomotive to save his life.

7. The careless fellow has forgotten _____ the door.

8. Our orders were _____ against the enemy at daybreak.

9. Commodore Dewey did not hesitate _____ into Manila Bay.

10. The performing bear stood up on his hind legs and began _____ clumsily.

III.

Underline the infinitives.

1. Lord Craven did me the honor to inquire for me by name.

2. Distress at last forced him to leave the country.

3. I know not what to think of it.

4. Our next care was to bring this booty home without meeting with the enemy.

5. To see judiciously requires no small skill in the seer.

6. The business of his own life is to dine.

7. The ladies are to fling nosegays; the court poets to scatter verses; the spectators are to be all in full dress.

8. Vathek invited the old man to dine, and even to remain some days in the palace.

9. Earth seemed to sink beneath, and heaven above to fall.

Chapter 101: Participles

Examples of participles and the noun or pronoun they modify may be seen in the following sentences:

> *Walking* up to the front door, *I* rang the bell.
> > [*Walking* modifies *I*]
> The policeman saw a *man sitting* on the steps.
> > [*sitting* modifies *man*]
> He observed a fine *dog stretched* out on the hearth rug.
> > [*stretched* modifies *dog*]
> He tripped over a *rope extended* across his path.
> > [*extended* modifies *rope*]

In the following sentences **circle** the participles. **Underline** the noun or pronoun that it modifies.

1. I see trees laden with ripening fruit.

2. In the green churchyard there were cattle tranquilly reposing upon the verdant graves.

3. The mob came roaring out, and thronged the place.

4. The girls sat weeping in silence.

5. Asked for a groat, he gives a thousand pounds.

6. Edward marched through Scotland at the head of a powerful army, compelling all ranks of people to submit to him.

7. The blackest desperation now gathers over him, broken only by red lightnings of remorse.

8. Arrived at Athens, soon he came to court.

9. Still the vessel went bounding onward.

10. Enchanted with the whole scene, I lingered on my voyage.

11. So saying, from the pavement he half rose

    Slowly, with pain, reclining on his arm,

    And looking wistfully with wide blue eyes

    As in a picture.

12. I went home that evening greatly oppressed in my mind, irresolute, and not knowing what to do.

13. Methinks I see thee straying on the beach.

14. A mountain stood

    Threatening from high,

    and overlooked the wood.

15. The wondering stranger round him gazed.

16. The castaways haunted the shore of the little island, always straining their eyes in the vain hope that a ship might show itself on the horizon.

17. Jack said nothing, but stood looking quizzically at his cousin.

18. Hearing of the disaster, they had come to my assistance.

19. At the first fire, twenty or thirty of the assailants fell dead or wounded.

20. Egbert stood motionless, horrified at the sight.

21. Almost exhausted, and swimming with the greatest difficulty, Philip reached the pier at last.

22. I found him hiding behind a tree.

Chapter 102: Present Participle

There are no written exercises for chapter 102.

Chapter 103: Past Participle of Weak Verbs

I.

Write, as in Section 436:

 (1) the same sentences with the verbs changed to the preterite (past);

 (2) the same sentences containing the past participle of each verb preceded by *was* or *has*.
  Thus,

PRESENT	PRETERITE	PAST PARTICIPLE
John *ties* his horse.	John *tied* his horse.	John's horse was *tied*. OR John has *tied* his horse.

1. The farmer sows his seed.

*Preterite*_____

*Past Participle*_____

2. The maid sets the table.

*Preterite*_____

*Past Participle*_____

3. The dog obeys his master.

*Preterite*_____

*Past Participle*_____

4. The pupil answers the question.

*Preterite*_____

*Past Participle*_____

5. The girl reads her book.

*Preterite*_____

*Past Participle*_____

6. He spends his money freely.

*Preterite*_____

*Past Participle*_____

7. He feels sorry for his faults.

*Preterite*_____

*Past Participle*_____

II.
Give the present, the preterite (past tense), and the past participle of each verb.

	PRESENT	PRETERITE (PAST)	PAST PARTICIPLE
1. quarrel			
2. accept			
3. tell			
4. offer			
5. hit			
6. drown			
7. flee			
8. start			
9. arrive			
10. hear			
11. convey			
12. sleep			
13. obey			
14. cut			
15. delay			

	PRESENT	PRETERITE (PAST)	PAST PARTICIPLE
16. sweep			
17. sell			
18. stay			
19. feel			
20. make			
21. deal			
22. beseech			
23. creep			
24. bring			
25. shut			
26. cast			
27. keep			
28. lose			
29. catch			
30. cost			
31. leave			

Chapter 104: Past Participle of Strong Verbs

Errors in the forms of the preterite (past) and the past participle are very common among careless speakers. Most of the erroneous forms now heard were once in good use, but this does not make them correct now.[3]

I.

Write in three columns, as in Section 437,

(1) the same sentences with the verbs changed to the preterite (past);

(2) sentences containing the past participle of each verb preceded by *was* or *has*. Thus,

PRESENT	PRETERITE	PAST PARTICIPLE
Jack *wears* no hat.	Jack *wore* no hat.	No hat was *worn* by Jack OR Jack has *worn* no hat.

1. Nobody knows the truth of the matter.

*Preterite*_____

*Past Participle*_____

2. Henry writes to his mother every day.

*Preterite*_____

*Past Participle*_____

3. The arrow strikes the target near the center.

*Preterite*_____

*Past Participle*_____

4. The explosion throws down the wall.

*Preterite*_____

*Past Participle*_____

---

[3] See the appendix for the correct modern forms.

5. January 1, 1901, begins a new century.

*Preterite*_____

Past Participle _____

6. The boy stands on the burning deck.

*Preterite*_____

Past Participle _____

7. A great banquet takes place tonight.

*Preterite*_____

Past Participle _____

8. The old man sits in the sun.

*Preterite*_____

Past Participle _____

9. The Mexican swings the lasso round his head.

*Preterite*_____

Past Participle _____

10. Johnson swims in the lake every day.

*Preterite*_____

Past Participle _____

II.

Make sentences containing each verb listed in bold print in:
- (1) the preterite (past)
- (2) the past participle (preceded by *have* or *has*)

<u>Set A</u>

begin

*Preterite*_____

Past Participle _____

drink

*Preterite*_____

*Past Participle*_____

ring

*Preterite*_____

Past Participle _____

run

*Preterite*_____

Past Participle _____

shrink

*Preterite*_____

Past Participle _____

sing

*Preterite*_____

Past Participle _____

sink

*Preterite*_____

Past Participle _____

spring

*Preterite*_____

*Past Participle*_____

swim

*Preterite*_____

*Past Participle*_____

Set B

bear

*Preterite*_____

*Past Participle*_____

bite

*Preterite*_____

*Past Participle*_____

break

*Preterite*_____

*Past Participle*_____

choose

*Preterite*_____

*Past Participle*_____

drive

*Preterite*_____

*Past Participle*_____

eat

*Preterite*_____

*Past Participle*_____

fall

*Preterite*_____

*Past Participle*_____

forget

*Preterite*_____

*Past Participle*_____

freeze

*Preterite*_____

*Past Participle*_____

hide

*Preterite*_____

*Past Participle*_____

ride

*Preterite*_____

*Past Participle*_____

shake

*Preterite*_____

*Past Participle*_____

speak

*Preterite*_____

*Past Participle*_____

steal

*Preterite*_____

*Past Participle*_____

swear

*Preterite*_____

*Past Participle*_____

take

*Preterite*_____

*Past Participle*_____

tear

*Preterite*_____

*Past Participle*_____

wear

*Preterite*_____

*Past Participle*_____

Chapter 105: Modifiers and Object of Infinitive or Participle

I.
In each of the following sentences insert an **adverb** or **adverbial phrase** to modify the infinitive.

1. I resolved to return _____ to England.

2. His orders to me were to keep him _____ in sight.

3. My first thought was to flee _____.

4. To rush _____ towards her was my impulse.

5. What right have you, then, to upbraid me _____ for having told you the

    truth?

6. The young man began to spend his money _____.

II.
Circle the participles, and **draw an arrow** to the noun or pronoun each modifies.
Underline all the modifiers and objects of the participles. The first one is done for you.

1. He occupied a farm of seventy acres, situated on the skirts of that pretty little village.

    > participle: *situated*   modifies: *farm*
    > modifiers of *situated*: <u>on the skirts of that pretty little village</u>

2. Mine was a small chamber, near the top of the house, fronting on the sea.

3. The listening crowd admire the lofty sound!

4. This life, which seems so fair,

    Is like a bubble blown up in the air.

5. Still is the toiling hand of Care;

    The panting herds repose.

6. His bridge was only loose planks laid upon large trestles.

7. She had a little room in the garret, where the maids heard her walking and sobbing at night.

8. The kind creature retreated into the garden, overcome with emotions.

9. The colonel, strengthened with some troops of horse from Yorkshire, comes up to the bridge.

10. Exhausted, I lay down at the base of the pyramid.

Chapter 106: Principal Parts of Verbs

Using the sentences from chapter 105, Exercise II, which are reproduced below, complete the following tasks:

1. **Underline** all the subjects **once** and the present and past tense verbs **twice.**
2. **Circle** all the present and past participles and **draw an arrow** to the substantive which each modifies.
3. **Label** whether the verb is weak with **W** or strong with **S** in each case.
4. **Write** the principal parts of every verb on the lines provided.

1. He occupied a farm of seventy acres, situated on the skirts of that pretty little village.

_____

_____

_____

2. Mine was a small chamber, near the top of the house, fronting on the sea.

_____

_____

_____

3. The listening crowd admire the lofty sound!

_____

_____

_____

4. This life, which seems so fair,

   Is like a bubble blown up in the air.

_____

_____

_____

5. Still is the toiling hand of Care;

The panting herds repose.

_____

_____

_____

6. His bridge was only loose planks laid upon large trestles.

_____

_____

_____

7. She had a little room in the garret, where the maids heard her walking and sobbing at

night.

_____

_____

_____

8. The kind creature retreated into the garden, overcome with emotions.

_____

_____

_____

9. The colonel, strengthened with some troops of horse from Yorkshire, comes up to the

bridge.

_____

_____

_____

10. Exhausted, I lay down at the base of the pyramid.

_____

_____

_____

Chapter 107: Verbal Nouns Ending in *-ing* (Gerunds)

In the following sentences **underline** all the words ending in *-ing* and **label** present participles with **PP** and verbal nouns with **VN**.

1. Books, painting, fiddling, and shooting were my amusements.

2. We are terribly afraid of Prince Eugene's coming.

3. Upon hearing my name, the old gentleman stepped up.

4. After I had resided at college seven years, my father died and left me — his blessing.

5. The neighing of the generous horse was heard.

6. Joseph still continued a huge clattering with the poker.

7. Then came the question of paying.

8. The day had been spent by the king in sport and feasting, and by the conspirators in preparing for their enterprise.

9. He first learned to write by imitating printed books.

10. Here we had the pleasure of breaking our fast on the leg of an old hare, and some broiled crows.

Chapter 108: Future Tense

I.

In the blanks provided, express the thought in each of the following sentences by means of a verb phrase with *will* or *shall*. First decide if the statement indicates simple futurity or if it is a statement of promise or determination. Some of the sentences have hints to get you started.

Futurity		*Promise or Determination*	
I shall	You will	I will	You shall
We shall	He/She/It will	We will	He/She/It shall
	They will		They shall

1. I am determined to learn my lesson. (*I will?* or *I shall?*)

   _____

2. I am willing to accompany you. (*Will* or *shall?*)

   _____

3. You are sure to fall if you climb that tree. (*You will* or *you shall?*)

   _____

4. I am sure to fall if I climb that tree. (*I will* or *I shall?*)

   _____

5. He is not to go home till he has learned his lesson. (*He will not* or *he shall not?*)

   _____

6. We agree to lend you fifty dollars. (*We will lend* or *we shall lend?*)

   _____

7. We are going to lend you fifty dollars, as a matter of fact. (*We will* or *we shall?*)

   _____

8. We are determined to find the rascal who stole our dog.

   _____

9. We are certain to succeed in the search.

_____

10. Columbus cannot fail to discover land if he sails on.

_____

11. You are resolved to win this game, I see.

_____

12. Are you willing to help me? *(Will you? or Shall you?)*

_____

13. Are you to be punished? *(Will you? or Shall you?)*

_____

14. Are we to be punished? *(Will we? or Shall we?)*

_____

II.
Fill in the blanks with **shall** or **will** as the sense requires. In some cases either may be used.

1. I _____ lose my train if I stay any longer.

2. I _____ be tired to death by night.

3. We _____ break through the ice if we are not careful.

4. We _____ try to do our duty.

5. We _____ not be guilty of such a crime.

6. We _____ give you what you need.

7. I _____ send a letter to him at once, since you wish it.

8. "I _____ drown!" cried the poor fellow, who was struggling in the water.

   "Nobody _____ help me!"

9. He _____ misspell his words, in spite of all I can say.

10. They _____ not be captured if I can help it.

11. They _____ catch nothing if they fish in that stream.

12. I _____ catch one fish if I have to stay here all day.

13. I _____ catch cold in this carriage.

14. I _____ ride as fast as I can.

Chapter 109: Passive Voice

I.

Underline the passive voice verbs. **Complete the chart** for each sentence, identifying the subject, verb phrase, verb tense, person (circle the correct choice) and number (circle the correct choice).

Example:
The ship <u>had been driven</u> on the rocks.

Subject	**ship**		
Verb phrase	**had been driven**		
Verb tense	**transitive, pluperfect tense**		
Person	first	second	**third**
Number	**singular**	plural	

1. The spears are uplifted; the matches are lit.

Subject			
Verb phrase			
Verb tense			
Person	first	second	third
Number	singular	plural	

2. Burton was staggered by this news.

Subject			
Verb phrase			
Verb tense			
Person	first	second	third
Number	singular	plural	

3. Thus was Corinth lost and won.

Subject			
Verb phrase			
Verb tense			
Person	first	second	third
Number	singular	plural	

4. Five hundred carpenters had been set at work.

Subject			
Verb phrase			
Verb tense			
Person	first	second	third
Number	singular	plural	

5. Old Simon is carried to his cottage door.

Subject			
Verb phrase			
Verb tense			
Person	first	second	third
Number	singular	plural	

6. You will be surprised at her good spirits.

Subject			
Verb phrase			
Verb tense			
Person	first	second	third
Number	singular	plural	

7. George Brand was ushered into the little drawing room.

Subject			
Verb phrase			
Verb tense			
Person	first	second	third
Number	singular	plural	

8. We shall be hit by the sharpshooters.

Subject			
Verb phrase			
Verb tense			
Person	first	second	third
Number	singular	plural	

9. The house had been struck by lightning.

Subject			
Verb phrase			
Verb tense			
Person	first	second	third
Number	singular	plural	

10. The art of writing had just been introduced into Arabia.

Subject			
Verb phrase			
Verb tense			
Person	first	second	third
Number	singular	plural	

11. They are bred up in the principles of honor and justice.

Subject			
Verb phrase			
Verb tense			
Person	first	second	third
Number	singular	plural	

12. He was carried away captive by the Indians.

Subject			
Verb phrase			
Verb tense			
Person	first	second	third
Number	singular	plural	

13. The alarm bell will be rung when the foe appears.

Subject			
Verb phrase			
Verb tense			
Person	first	second	third
Number	singular	plural	

14. For my own part, I swam as Fortune directed me, and was pushed forward by wind and

tide.

Subject			
Verb phrase			
Verb tense			
Person	first	second	third
Number	singular	plural	

15. Thus the emperor's great palace was built.

Subject			
Verb phrase			
Verb tense			
Person	first	second	third
Number	singular	plural	

16. The stranger was surrounded, pinioned with strong fetters, and hurried away to the prison of the great tower.

Subject			
Verb phrase			
Verb tense			
Person	first	second	third
Number	singular	plural	

17. Some of the cargo had been damaged by the sea water.

Subject			
Verb phrase			
Verb tense			
Person	first	second	third
Number	singular	plural	

18. Our blows were dealt at random.

Subject			
Verb phrase			
Verb tense			
Person	first	second	third
Number	singular	plural	

19. Nothing will be gained by hurry.

Subject			
Verb phrase			
Verb tense			
Person	first	second	third
Number	singular	plural	

20. I shall be surprised if he succeeds.

Subject			
Verb phrase			
Verb tense			
Person	first	second	third
Number	singular	plural	

21. The orchards were hewn down.

Subject			
Verb phrase			
Verb tense			
Person	first	second	third
Number	singular	plural	

22. Panama was captured by Morgan, the buccaneer.

Subject			
Verb phrase			
Verb tense			
Person	first	second	third
Number	singular	plural	

23. The bridge will be swept away by the flood.

Subject			
Verb phrase			
Verb tense			
Person	first	second	third
Number	singular	plural	

24. My efforts had been rewarded with success.

Subject			
Verb phrase			
Verb tense			
Person	first	second	third
Number	singular	plural	

25. The bank was robbed last night.

Subject			
Verb phrase			
Verb tense			
Person	first	second	third
Number	singular	plural	

II.

Use in sentences some **passive** form of each of the following verbs:

1. delay _____

2. devour _____

3. pierce _____

4. set _____

5. send _____

6. bring _____

7. betray _____

8. fulfill _____

9. declare _____

10. conduct _____

11. guide _____

12. spend _____

13. read_____

14. feel_____

15. catch _____

16. sink _____

17. cut _____

18. find _____

19. steal_____

20. drink_____

21. ring _____

Chapter 110: Active and Passive

I.
Change the active verbs to the passive voice without changing the meaning of the sentences. Note that the object of the active verb becomes the subject of the passive.

1. Theseus killed the Minotaur.

    _____

2. Fulton invented steamboats.

    _____

3. The President will veto the bill.

    _____

4. Dampier explored the coast of Australia.

    _____

5. The Normans conquered the Saxons.

    _____

6. A band of Indians attacked Deerfield.

    _____

7. A storm has disabled the fleet.

    _____

8. The miner had found gold in the bed of the stream.

    _____

9. John Greenleaf Whittier wrote "Snow-Bound."

    _____

10. The sun will soon melt the snow.

    _____

11. Edison invented the incandescent electric light.

_____

12. The Romans conquered Spain.

_____

13. The French settled Louisiana.

_____

14. The Dutch colonized New York.

_____

15. Bruce defeated the English at Bannockburn.

_____

16. An English court declared Sir William Wallace guilty of treason.

_____

17. Henry V defeated the French at Agincourt.

_____

18. The Indians outwitted General Braddock.

_____

19. Braddock had scorned Washington's advice.

_____

20. The Angles and Saxons invaded and subdued Britain.

_____

II.

Analyze the sentences from chapter 109, Exercise I, reproduced below.

1. **Underline** complete subject **once** and complete predicate **twice**.
2. **Label** simple subject with **S** and simple predicate with **V**.
3. Place **parentheses** around phrases and brackets around clauses.
4. **Label** the parts of prepositional phrases with **Prep** for prepositions and **OP** for objects of the preposition.
5. **Label** any predicate adjectives with **PA** and predicate nominatives with **PN**.
6. **Label** any direct objects with **DO** and indirect objects with **IO**.
7. **Label** modifiers (adverbs **Adv**, adjectives **Adj**, adverb clauses **Adv**, adjective clauses **Adj**).

1. The spears are uplifted; the matches are lit.

2. Burton was staggered by this news.

3. Thus was Corinth lost and won.

4. Five hundred carpenters had been set at work.

5. Old Simon is carried to his cottage door.

6. You will be surprised at her good spirits.

7. George Brand was ushered into the little drawing room.

8. We shall be hit by the sharpshooters.

9. The house had been struck by lightning.

10. The art of writing had just been introduced into Arabia.

11. They are bred up in the principles of honor and justice.

12. He was carried away captive by the Indians.

13. The alarm bell will be rung when the foe appears.

14. For my own part, I swam as Fortune directed me, and was pushed forward by wind and

   tide.

15. Thus the emperor's great palace was built.

16. The stranger was surrounded, pinioned with strong fetters, and hurried away to the prison

   of the great tower.

17. Some of the cargo had been damaged by the sea water.

18. Our blows were dealt at random.

19. Nothing will be gained by hurry.

20. I shall be surprised if he succeeds.

21. The orchards were hewn down.

22. Panama was captured by Morgan, the buccaneer.

23. The bridge will be swept away by the flood.

24. My efforts had been rewarded with success.

25. The bank was robbed last night.

Do you notice a sentence pattern in a majority of these sentences? Describe the pattern here:

_____

_____

Chapter 111: Complete or Compound Tense

I.

In the following sentences **underline** all the verbs. **Complete the chart** for each sentence, identifying the subject, verb phrase, verb tense, person (circle the correct choice) and number (circle the correct choice).

1. My eldest daughter had finished her Latin lessons, and my son had finished his Greek.

Subject			
Verb phrase			
Verb tense			
Person	first	second	third
Number	singular	plural	

Subject			
Verb phrase			
Verb tense			
Person	first	second	third
Number	singular	plural	

2. There has been a heavy thunderstorm this afternoon.

Subject			
Verb phrase			
Verb tense			
Person	first	second	third
Number	singular	plural	

3. A multitude of humming birds had been attracted thither.

Subject			
Verb phrase			
Verb tense			
Person	first	second	third
Number	singular	plural	

4. Our men had besieged some fortified house near Oxford.

Subject			
Verb phrase			
Verb tense			
Person	first	second	third
Number	singular	plural	

5. I really have had enough of fighting.

Subject			
Verb phrase			
Verb tense			
Person	first	second	third
Number	singular	plural	

6. All shyness and embarrassment had vanished.

Subject			
Verb phrase			
Verb tense			
Person	first	second	third
Number	singular	plural	

7. The great tree has been undermined by winter floods.

Subject			
Verb phrase			
Verb tense			
Person	first	second	third
Number	singular	plural	

8. He had lost his way in the pine woods.

Subject			
Verb phrase			
Verb tense			
Person	first	second	third
Number	singular	plural	

9. Thousands had sunk on the ground overpowered.

Subject			
Verb phrase			
Verb tense			
Person	first	second	third
Number	singular	plural	

10. A storm of mingled rain and snow had come on.

Subject			
Verb phrase			
Verb tense			
Person	first	second	third
Number	singular	plural	

11. We had left our two servants behind us at Calais.

Subject			
Verb phrase			
Verb tense			
Person	first	second	third
Number	singular	plural	

12. The patience of Scotland had found an end at last.

Subject			
Verb phrase			
Verb tense			
Person	first	second	third
Number	singular	plural	

13. His passion has cast a mist before his sense.

Subject			
Verb phrase			
Verb tense			
Person	first	second	third
Number	singular	plural	

14. The surgeon has set my arm very skillfully and well.

Subject			
Verb phrase			
Verb tense			
Person	first	second	third
Number	singular	plural	

15. A strange golden moonlight had crept up the skies.

Subject			
Verb phrase			
Verb tense			
Person	first	second	third
Number	singular	plural	

16. You will have finished your task by Saturday.

Subject			
Verb phrase			
Verb tense			
Person	first	second	third
Number	singular	plural	

17. The wind has howled all day.

Subject			
Verb phrase			
Verb tense			
Person	first	second	third
Number	singular	plural	

18. He had gasped out a few incoherent words.

Subject			
Verb phrase			
Verb tense			
Person	first	second	third
Number	singular	plural	

II.
Underline the infinitives and the participles. Use the lines provided to **parse** them by writing the tense of each infinitive (present or perfect) and of each participle (present, past, or perfect).

1. Columbus's crew had begun to despair._____

2. I should like to have seen his face when he heard this news. _____

3. I ought to have known that the lizard was harmless._____

4. 'T is better to have loved and lost _____

   Than never to have loved at all._____

5. Having done my best, I am ready to endure whatever comes._____

   _____

6. Having once suffered from the bite of a tarantula, Johnson was very much afraid even of

   harmless spiders. _____

Chapter 112: Progressive Verb Phrases, Part I

There are no written exercises for chapter 112.

Chapter 113: Progressive Verb Phrases, Part II

Double underline the verbs and verb phrases. **Parse** them by writing on the line provided:
1. tense
2. progressive or not?

The first one is done for you.

1. The church bells, with various tones, but all in harmony, <u><u>were calling</u></u> out and <u><u>responding</u></u>

   to one another. *were calling/were responding: past tense, progressive form*

2. A huge load of oak wood was passing through the gateway. _____

3. Many a chapel bell the hour is telling. _____

4. Edmund was standing thoughtfully by the fire. _____

5. A thick mist was gradually spreading over every object. _____

6. I have been walking by the river. _____

7. Merry it is in the good greenwood _____

   When the mavis and merle are singing. _____

   When the deer sweeps by, and the hounds are in cry, _____

   And the hunter's horn is ringing. _____

8. The morn is laughing in the sky. _____

9. Curly-headed urchins are gambolling before the door. _____

Chapter 114: Emphatic Verb Phrases

Change the progressive and the emphatic forms to the ordinary tense forms. **Tell** which of the "emphatic" forms are really emphatic.

1. The wind did blow, the cloak did fly.

_____

2. Glossy bees at noon do fieldward pass.

_____

3. A second time did Matthew stop.

_____

4. He did come rather earlier than had been expected.

_____

5. She did look a little hot and disconcerted for a few minutes.

_____

6. The dogs did bark, the children screamed,

    Up flew the windows all.

_____

_____

7. Our true friends do not always praise us.

_____

8. But Knowledge to their eyes her ample page,

    Rich with the spoils of time, did ne'er unroll.

_____

_____

9. Beasts did leap and birds did sing,

    Trees did grow and plants did spring.

    _____

    _____

10. The noise of the wind and of the thunder did not awaken the king, for he was old and

    weary with his journey.

    _____

    _____

11. Why did you not tell me the news?

    _____

12. I did tell you everything that I had heard.

    _____

13. Where does Mr. Jackson live? I do not know.

    _____

14. You did give me some anxiety by your long absence.

    _____

15. Does this train go to Chicago?

    _____

16. The conductor says that it does.

    _____

17. I did not believe that Jones was guilty of intentional falsehood; but I did think that he was

    rather careless in his account of what took place.

    _____

    _____

18. What did he tell you about Thomas?

    _____

Chapter 115: Imperative Mood

In each of the following imperative sentences **double underline** the verb in the imperative mood. **Underline** the subject **once**, when it is expressed; when not, supply it by writing it on the line provided.

1. _____Let us have a walk through Kensington Gardens.

2. _____Do not forget the poor.

3. _____Hope not, base man, unquestioned hence to go!

4. _____Would ye be blest? _____ Despise low joys, low gains.

5. _____Summon Colonel Atherton without a moment's delay.

6. _____Look up and be not afraid, but hold forth thy hand.

7. _____Mount ye! spur ye! _____ skirr the plain!

8. _____O, listen, listen, ladies gay!

9. _____Toll ye the churchbell sad and slow.

10. _____You, Herbert and Luffness, alight,

    And bind the wounds of yonder knight.

11. _____Stay with us. _____ Go not to Wittenberg.

12. _____Listen to the rolling thunder.

13. _____Call off your dogs!

14. _____Keep thine elbow from my side, friend.

15. _____Do not leave me to perish in this wilderness.

16. _____Saddle my horses! _____ Call my train together.

Chapter 115: Additional Review Exercise[4]

You have now studied the inflections of the verb in the **indicative mood** (that is, in the set of forms used in most sentences) and the **imperative mood**. You are acquainted with the **present, preterite,** and **future tenses;** with the **complete tenses;** with the **infinitive** and **participle;** with the **progressive** and **emphatic verb phrases.** You have learned to distinguish **person** and **number**.

In the following passages **double underline** the verbs and verb phrases and **parse** them by telling all you can about the form and construction of each verb in the line provided. Write the:
   1. tense (or if it is an infinitive or participle, progressive or emphatic verb phrase)
   2. voice (active or passive) and mood (indicative or imperative),
   3. person (first, second, third)
   4. number (singular or plural).

1. The more I give to thee, the more I have.

2. Comes the king back from Wales?

3. Dost thou not hear them call?

4. The more we stay, the stronger grows our foe.

5. I know not, gentlemen, what you intend.

6. How long hast thou to serve, Francis?

7. A great portion of my time was passed in a deep and mournful silence.

---

[4] Here chapters 90-115 should be reviewed.

8. The day, which had been tempestuous, was succeeded by a heavy and settled rain.

_____

9. His courage was not staggered, even for an instant.

_____

10. I was startled by the sound of trumpets.

_____

(Chapter 115 exercise continued on next page.)

11. The company was surprised to see the old man so merry, when suffering such great losses; and the Mandarin himself, coming out, asked him, how he, who had grieved so much, and given way to calamity the day before, could now be so cheerful?

_____

_____

_____

_____

"You ask me one question," cries the old man; "Let me answer by asking another: Which is the more durable, a hard thing or a soft thing; that which resists or that which makes no resistance?"

_____

_____

_____

_____

"A hard thing, to be sure," replied the Mandarin.

There you are wrong," returned Shingfu. "I am now four-score years old; and, if you look in my mouth, you will find that I have lost all my teeth, but not a bit of my tongue."

_____

_____

_____

_____

Chapter 116: Nominative Absolute

I.

In the following sentences **underline** all nouns in the absolute construction and **underline** the participle in agreement. Mark above the participle whether each expresses the time with **T**, place with **P**, or circumstance of the action with **C**.

1. Navigation was at a stop, our ships neither coming in nor going out as before.

2. Night coming on, we sought refuge from the gathering storm.

3. The song ended, she hastily relinquished her seat to another lady.

4. The house consisted of seven rooms, the dairy and cellar included.

5. The resolution being thus taken, they set out the next day.

6. They had some difficulty in passing the ferry at the riverside, the ferryman being afraid of

   them.

7. She sat beneath the birchen tree,

   Her elbow resting on her knee.

8. The signal of battle being given with two cannon shot, we marched in order of battalia

   down the hill.

9. The dark lead-colored ocean lay stretched before them, its dreary expanse concealed by

   lowering clouds.

10. Next Anger rushed, his eyes on fire.

11. The last of these voyages not proving very fortunate, I grew weary of the sea.

12. The two Scottish generals, Macbeth and Banquo, returning victorious from this great battle,

    their way lay over a blasted heath.

13. The cottage was situated in a valley, the hills being for the most part crowned with rich and verdant foliage, their sides covered with vineyards and corn, and a clear, transparent rivulet murmuring along from east to west.

14. This done, the conspirators separated.

15. This being understood, the next step is easily taken.

16. This said, he picked up his pack and trudged on.

II.

Analyze the sentences in Exercise I, reproduced below. Remember that nominative absolutes modify the predicate.

1. **Underline** complete subject **once** and complete predicate **twice**.
2. **Label** simple subject with **S** and simple predicate with **V**.
3. **Label** any predicate adjectives with **PA** and predicate nominatives with **PN**.
4. Offset phrases with **(parentheses)** and clauses with **[brackets]**.
5. **Label** the nominative absolute phrase **NA phrase**, and within the phrase label the noun **NA** and the participle in agreement **NAP**.
6. **Label** any direct objects with **DO** and indirect objects **IO**.
7. **Label** modifiers (adverbs **Adv**, adjectives **Adj**, adverb clauses **Adv**, and adjective clauses **Adj**) and conjunctions with **C**.

1. Navigation was at a stop, our ships neither coming in nor going out as before.

2. Night coming on, we sought refuge from the gathering storm.

3. The song ended, she hastily relinquished her seat to another lady.

4. The house consisted of seven rooms, the dairy and cellar included.

5. The resolution being thus taken, they set out the next day.

6. They had some difficulty in passing the ferry at the riverside, the ferryman being afraid of

them.

7. She sat beneath the birchen tree,

Her elbow resting on her knee.

8. The signal of battle being given with two cannon-shot, we marched in order of battalia

down the hill.

9. The dark lead-colored ocean lay stretched before them, its dreary expanse concealed by

lowering clouds.

10. Next Anger rushed, his eyes on fire.

11. The last of these voyages not proving very fortunate, I grew weary of the sea.

12. The two Scottish generals, Macbeth and Banquo, returning victorious from this great battle,

their way lay over a blasted heath.

(Chapter 116 exercise continued on next page.)

13. The cottage was situated in a valley, the hills being for the most part crowned with rich and

verdant foliage, their sides covered with vineyards and corn, and a clear, transparent

rivulet murmuring along from east to west.

14. This done, the conspirators separated.

15. This being understood, the next step is easily taken.

16. This said, he picked up his pack and trudged on.

Chapter 117: Cognate Object and Adverbial Objective

Underline the cognate objects and the adverbial objectives, and **parse** each of them by writing on the line:

1. the noun class (common or proper),
2. gender (M, F, or N),
3. number (S, P),
4. case,
5. cognate object or adverbial objective?

EXAMPLES:

Jane laughed a merry *laugh*.

Laugh: common noun, neuter gender, singular number, objective case; cognate object of the verb *laughed*.

The messenger ran three *miles*.

Miles: common noun, neuter gender, plural number, objective case; adverbial objective modifying *ran*.

1. But the skipper blew a whiff from his pipe,

    and a scornful laugh laughed he.

    _____

2. The wind blew a gale.

    _____

3. Everybody looked daggers at the intruder.

    _____

4. Speak the speech, I pray you, as I pronounce it to you.

    _____

5. The hail was terrific. The sky seemed to rain stones.

    _____

6. The colonists endured oppression a long time.

    _____

7. The poet Gray worked upon his "Elegy" several years.

_____

8. That mountain is distant five miles from this spot.

_____

9. The soldiers marched Indian file.

_____

10. The table is six feet long, four feet wide, and three feet high.

_____

11. I cannot swim a yard farther.

_____

12. The cannon carried four miles.

_____

13. You will never accomplish anything that way.

_____

14. The road ran a very long distance without a curve.

_____

Chapter 118: Predicate Objective

I.
Fill in each blank with a **predicate** *objective*.

1. The boys elected Will Sampson _____ of the boat club.

2. I always thought your brother an excellent _____.

3. Do you call the man your _____?

4. The governor appointed Smith _____.

5. Everybody voted the talkative fellow a _____.

6. The pirates chose Judson _____.

7. The hunter called the animal a _____.

8. My parents named my brother _____.

9. I cannot think him such a _____.

10. The merchant's losses made him a poor _____.

11. You called my brother a _____.

II.
Fill in each blank with a **predicate** *adjective*.

1. A good son makes his mother _____.

2. The jury declares the prisoner _____.

3. This noise will surely drive me _____.

4. I cannot pronounce you _____ of this accusation.

5. The sedate burghers thought the gay youngster very _____.

6. The travelers thought the river _____.

7. Our elders often think our conduct _____.

8. I call the boy _____ for his age.

9. Exercise makes us _____.

10. Nothing makes one so _____ as a good dinner.

11. Do you pronounce the prisoner _____?

12. Do you think us _____?

III.

Analyze the sentences in I and II, reproduced below, by completing the following steps. (Your teacher may wish to have you diagram these sentences.)

1. **Identify** if the sentence is declarative, interrogative, imperative, or exclamatory by writing **D, Int, Imp,** or **Exc** in the blank on the left.
2. **Underline** the complete subject **once** and the complete predicate **twice.**
3. **Label** the simple subject with **S,** and the simple predicate with **V.**
4. **Label** the modifiers (**Adv, Adj**)
5. **Label** the direct object with **DO** and the transitive verb with **TV,** the predicate objective noun with **PO,** or predicate adjective used as predicate objective with **PO.**

Exercise I sentences:

1. _____The boys elected Will Sampson _____ of the boat club.

2. _____I always thought your brother an excellent _____.

3. _____Do you call the man your _____?

4. _____The governor appointed Smith _____.

5. _____Everybody voted the talkative fellow a _____.

6. _____The pirates chose Judson _____.

7. _____The hunter called the animal a _____.

8. _____My parents named my brother _____.

9. _____I cannot think him such a _____.

10. _____The merchant's losses made him a poor _____.

11. _____You called my brother a _____.

Exercise II sentences:

1. _____A good son makes his mother _____.

2. _____The jury declares the prisoner _____.

3. _____This noise will surely drive me _____.

4. _____I cannot pronounce you _____ of this accusation.

5. _____The sedate burghers thought the gay youngster very _____.

6. _____The travelers thought the river _____.

7. _____Our elders often think our conduct _____.

8. _____I call the boy _____ for his age.

9. _____Exercise makes us _____.

10. _____Nothing makes one so _____ as a good dinner.

11. _____Do you pronounce the prisoner _____?

12. _____Do you think us _____?

IV.

Underline and label:

      (1) transitive verbs with **TV**,

      (2) direct objects with **DO**, and

      (3) predicate objectives with **PO**.

1. Pope had now declared himself a poet.

2. The people call it a backward year.

3. He called them untaught knaves.

4. He could make a small town a great city.

5. She called him the best child in the world.

6. A man must be born a poet, but he may make himself an orator.

7. Fear of death makes many a man a coward.

8. Ye call me chief.

9. The Poles always elected some nobleman their king.

10. He cared not, indeed, that the world should call him a miser; he cared not that the world

    should call him a churl; he cared not that the world should call him odd.

V.

The **predicate objective** becomes a **predicate nominative** when the verb is changed from the **active** voice to the **passive.**

ACTIVE VOICE	PASSIVE VOICE
(Predicate Objective)	*(Predicate Nominative)*
The people elected Grant *president.*	Grant was elected *president* by the people.
I named my dog *Jack.*	My dog was named *Jack.*
They think such conduct *unwise.*	Such conduct is thought *unwise.*
The noise drove me *mad.*	I was driven *mad* by the noise.

Change the verbs in Exercises II and IV to the passive voice. They are reproduced for you.

What happens to the predicate objective or adjective? _____

Exercise II sentences:

1. A good son makes his mother _____.

   _____

2. The jury declares the prisoner _____.

   _____

3. This noise will surely drive me _____.

   _____

4. I cannot pronounce you _____ of this accusation.

   _____

5. The sedate burghers thought the gay youngster very _____.

   _____

6. The travelers thought the river _____.

   _____

7. Our elders often think our conduct _____.

   _____

8. I call the boy _____ for his age.

   _____

9. Exercise makes us _____.

   _____

10. Nothing makes one so _____ as a good dinner.

   _____

11. Do you pronounce the prisoner _____?

_____

12. Do you think us _____?

_____

Exercise IV sentences:

1. Pope had now declared himself a poet.

_____

2. The people call it a backward year.

_____

3. He called them untaught knaves.

_____

4. He could make a small town a great city.

_____

5. She called him the best child in the world.

_____

6. A man must be born a poet, but he may make himself an orator.

_____

7. Fear of death makes many a man a coward.

_____

8. Ye call me chief.

_____

9. The Poles always elected some nobleman their king.

_____

10. He cared not, indeed, that the world should call him a miser; he cared not that the world

should call him a churl; he cared not that the world should call him odd.

Chapter 119: Relative Pronouns

I.

In these sentences from chapter 51, Exercise III (reproduced below), **circle** all the relative pronouns. In the line provided, **write**:

> (1) their number (**S, P**), person (**1st, 2nd, 3rd**), and gender (**M, F, M/F, N**);
>
> (2) write their antecedents;
>
> (3) identify their case (**N, G, O**).

1. A sharp rattle was heard on the window, which made the children jump.

_____

2. The small torch that he held sent forth a radiance by which suddenly the whole surface of

   the desert was illuminated.

_____

3. He that has most time has none to lose.

_____

4. Gray rocks peeped from amidst the lichens and creeping plants which covered them as

   with a garment of many colors.

_____

5. The enclosed fields, which were generally forty feet square, resembled so many beds of

   flowers.

_____

6. They that reverence too much old times are but a scorn to the new.

_____

7. The morning came which was to launch me into the world, and from which my whole

   succeeding life has, in many important points, taken its coloring.

_____

8. Ten guineas, added to about two which I had remaining from my pocket money, seemed to me sufficient for an indefinite length of time.

_____

9. He is the freeman whom the truth makes free.

_____

10. There was one philosopher who chose to live in a tub.

_____

11. Conquerors are a class of men with whom, for the most part, the world could well dispense.

_____

12. The light came from a lamp that burned brightly on the table.

_____

13. The sluggish stream through which we moved yielded sullenly to the oar.

_____

14. The place from which the light proceeded was a small chapel.

_____

15. The warriors went into battle clad in complete armor, which covered them from top to toe.

_____

16. She seemed as happy as a wave

   That dances on the sea.

_____

17. He sang out a long, loud, and canorous peal of laughter, that might have wakened the Seven Sleepers.

_____

18. Thou hadst a voice whose sound was like the sea.

_____

19. Many of Douglas's followers were slain in the battle in which he himself fell.

_____

II.

Review your work in Exercise II, chapter 51. (The sentences from _The Mother Tongue Student Workbook 1_ are reproduced below. If you did not complete this in _Workbook 1_, you may fill in the missing relative pronouns now.) **Write** on the line provided why you used one relative rather than another.

1. The house _____ stands yonder belongs to Colonel Carton.

_____

2. Are you the man _____ saved my daughter from drowning?

_____

3. The sailor's wife gazed at the stately ship _____ was taking her husband away from

    her.

_____

4. A young farmer, _____ name was Judkins, was the first to enlist.

_____

5. Nothing _____ you can do will help me.

_____

6. The horses _____ belong to the squire are famous trotters.

_____

7. James Adams is the strongest man _____ I have ever seen.

_____

8. My friend, _____ we had overtaken on his way down town, greeted us cheerfully.

_____

9. Behold the man _____ the king delighteth to honor!

_____

10. That is the captain _____ ship was wrecked last December.

_____

III.
Make twelve sentences containing the pronouns given (some are listed twice).

1. who_____

2. whom_____

3. which_____

4. whose_____

5. of which_____

6. that_____

7. as_____

8. who_____

9. whom_____

10. which_____

11. whose_____

12. that_____

IV.

Fill in each blank in the sentence with the proper form of the copula (*am, is, are*). Write on the line provided the person **(1st, 2nd, 3rd)** and number (**S, P**) of the antecedent (which is italicized for you) in each sentence, and observe that the relative must agree with it.

1. You find fault with *me*, who _____ not to blame._____

2. *You* who _____ present are all members of the society. _____

3. *We* who _____ in good health should have sympathy for the sick. _____

4. *He* who _____ fond of good books will never feel lonely. _____

5. *Those* of you who _____ ready may start at once. _____

6. *I*, who _____ a poor swimmer, shall never win the prize. _____

7. *Nobody* who _____ young ever really expects old age._____

8. *Such* of us as _____ aware of the facts have little doubt of the man's innocence.

_____

Chapter 120: Gender of Relatives

There are no written exercises for chapter 120.

Chapter 121: Descriptive and Restrictive Relatives

In Exercises II and III from chapter 51. The sentences are reproduced below. Be sure to fill in the relatives again. Identify each relative as **descriptive** or **restrictive** and be prepared to tell why. **Label** the relative descriptive with **D** and restrictive with **R**.

Exercise II sentences:

1. The house _____ stands yonder belongs to Colonel Carton.

2. Are you the man _____ saved my daughter from drowning?

3. The sailor's wife gazed at the stately ship _____ was taking her husband away from her.

4. A young farmer, _____ name was Judkins, was the first to enlist.

5. Nothing _____ you can do will help me.

6. The horses _____ belong to the squire are famous trotters.

7. James Adams is the strongest man _____ I have ever seen.

8. My friend, _____ we had overtaken on his way down town, greeted us cheerfully.

9. Behold the man _____ the king delighteth to honor!

10. That is the captain _____ ship was wrecked last December.

Exercise III sentences:

1. A sharp rattle was heard on the window, which made the children jump.

2. The small torch that he held sent forth a radiance by which suddenly the whole surface of the desert was illuminated.

3. He that has most time has none to lose.

4. Gray rocks peeped from amidst the lichens and creeping plants which covered them as with a garment of many colors.

5. The enclosed fields, which were generally forty feet square, resembled so many beds of flowers.

6. They that reverence too much old times are but a scorn to the new.

7. The morning came which was to launch me into the world, and from which my whole succeeding life has, in many important points, taken its coloring.

8. Ten guineas, added to about two which I had remaining from my pocket money, seemed to me sufficient for an indefinite length of time.

9. He is the freeman whom the truth makes free.

10. There was one philosopher who chose to live in a tub.

11. Conquerors are a class of men with whom, for the most part, the world could well dispense.

12. The light came from a lamp that burned brightly on the table.

13. The sluggish stream through which we moved yielded sullenly to the oar.

14. The place from which the light proceeded was a small chapel.

15. The warriors went into battle clad in complete armor, which covered them from top to toe.

16. She seemed as happy as a wave

    That dances on the sea.

17. He sang out a long, loud, and canorous peal of laughter, that might have wakened the Seven Sleepers.

18. Thou hadst a voice whose sound was like the sea.

19. Many of Douglas's followers were slain in the battle in which he himself fell.

Chapter 122: The Relative Pronoun "What"

Change each *what* to *that which*. Explain the constructions of *that* and *which* (what job is it doing in the sentence, *e.g.* subject of subordinate clause or direct object of main clause).

1. We seldom imitate what we do not love.

_____

_____

2. He gives us what our wants require.

_____

_____

3. What's mine is yours, and what is yours is mine.

_____

_____

4. What you have said may be true.

_____

_____

5. What I have is at your service.

_____

_____

6. The spendthrift has wasted what his father laid up.

_____

_____

7. What I earn supports the family.

_____

_____

8. What supports the family is Tom's wages.

_____

_____

Chapter 123: Compound Relative Pronouns

There are no written exercises for chapter 123.

Chapter 124: Relative Adjectives and Adverbs

I.

In each of the following sentences **underline** the relatives and **explain** the construction of *that* and of *which*. (See Sections 518, 521, and 523 in your text.) Then change *that which* to *what* and explain the double construction of *what*.

1. That which man has done, man can do. _____

_____

_____

2. I will describe only that which I have seen. _____

_____

_____

3. That which was left was sold for old iron. _____

_____

_____

4. That which inspired the inventor was the hope of final success. _____

_____

_____

5. Captivity is that which I fear most. _____

_____

_____

6. That which we have, we prize not. That which we lack, we value. _____

_____

_____

7. I thought of that which the old sailor had told of storms and shipwrecks._____

_____

_____

8. Give careful heed to that which I say. _____

_____

_____

9. That which offended Bertram most was his cousin's sneer. _____

_____

_____

10. That which is done cannot be undone. _____

_____

_____

Oral Exercise: Substitute *whatever* for *that which* whenever you can.

II.
Underline the relatives and **explain** their construction (*e.g.* direct object of subordinate clause).

1. Whoever he is, I will loose his bonds.

_____

2. Give this message to whomever you see.

_____

3. Give this letter to anyone whom you see.

_____

4. Whatsoever he doeth shall prosper.

_____

5. Everything that he does shall prosper.

_____

6. I owe to you whatever success I have had.

_____

7. I owe to you any success that I have had.

_____

8. Whoever deserts you, I will remain faithful.

_____

9. He gave a full account of whatever he had seen.

_____

10. Whichever road you take, you will find it rough and lonely.

_____

Chapter 125: Interrogative Pronouns, Etc.

I.

Write fifteen interrogative sentences, using all the forms of the interrogative pronouns and adjectives.

Interrogative pronouns

1. who_____

2. which _____

3. what _____

4. whom _____

5. whose _____

Interrogative adjectives

6. which _____

7. what _____

Interrogative adverbs

8. where _____

9. when_____

10. whence_____

11. whither_____

12. how_____

13. why_____

Interrogative pronouns, adjectives, or adverbs of your choice

14. _____

15. _____

II.

For each sentence, **write** the interrogative pronoun in the blank and **circle** its gender, number, part of speech, and case in the chart provided. Remember that some interrogative pronouns could be masculine and feminine.

1. Who told you that I was going to London?

Interrogative pronoun

Gender	masculine	feminine	neuter
Number	singular	plural	
Part of speech	substantive	adjective	adverb
Case (if substantive)	nominative	objective	genitive
Noun modified (if adjective)			

2. What is the meaning of this terrible summons?

Interrogative pronoun

Gender	masculine	feminine	neuter
Number	singular	plural	
Part of speech	substantive	adjective	adverb
Case (if substantive)	nominative	objective	genitive
Noun modified (if adjective)			

3. Who are these strange-looking men?

Interrogative pronoun

Gender	masculine	feminine	neuter
Number	singular	plural	
Part of speech	substantive	adjective	adverb
Case (if substantive)	nominative	objective	genitive
Noun modified (if adjective)			

4. What dost thou want? Whence didst thou come?

Interrogative pronoun

Gender	masculine	feminine	neuter
Number	singular	plural	
Part of speech	substantive	adjective	adverb
Case (if substantive)	nominative	objective	genitive
Noun modified (if adjective)			

Interrogative pronoun

Gender	masculine	feminine	neuter
Number	singular	plural	
Part of speech	substantive	adjective	adverb
Case (if substantive)	nominative	objective	genitive
Noun modified (if adjective)			

5. What is the creature doing here?

Interrogative pronoun

Gender	masculine	feminine	neuter
Number	singular	plural	
Part of speech	substantive	adjective	adverb
Case (if substantive)	nominative	objective	genitive
Noun modified (if adjective)			

6. Which of you is William Tell?

Interrogative pronoun

Gender	masculine	feminine	neuter
Number	singular	plural	
Part of speech	substantive	adjective	adverb
Case (if substantive)	nominative	objective	genitive
Noun modified (if adjective)			

7. Where did we go on that memorable night? What did we see? What did we do? Or rather, what did we not see, and what did we not do?

Interrogative pronoun

Gender	masculine	feminine	neuter
Number	singular	plural	
Part of speech	substantive	adjective	adverb
Case (if substantive)	nominative	objective	genitive
Noun modified (if adjective)			

Interrogative pronoun

Gender	masculine	feminine	neuter
Number	singular	plural	
Part of speech	substantive	adjective	adverb
Case (if substantive)	nominative	objective	genitive
Noun modified (if adjective)			

Interrogative pronoun

Gender	masculine	feminine	neuter
Number	singular	plural	
Part of speech	substantive	adjective	adverb
Case (if substantive)	nominative	objective	genitive
Noun modified (if adjective)			

Interrogative pronoun

Gender	masculine	feminine	neuter
Number	singular	plural	
Part of speech	substantive	adjective	adverb
Case (if substantive)	nominative	objective	genitive
Noun modified (if adjective)			

8. Of what crime am I accused? Where are the witnesses?

Interrogative pronoun

Gender	masculine	feminine	neuter
Number	singular	plural	
Part of speech	substantive	adjective	adverb
Case (if substantive)	nominative	objective	genitive
Noun modified (if adjective)			

Interrogative pronoun

Gender	masculine	feminine	neuter
Number	singular	plural	
Part of speech	substantive	adjective	adverb
Case (if substantive)	nominative	objective	genitive
Noun modified (if adjective)			

9. Whom shall you invite to the wedding?

Interrogative pronoun

Gender	masculine	feminine	neuter
Number	singular	plural	
Part of speech	substantive	adjective	adverb
Case (if substantive)	nominative	objective	genitive
Noun modified (if adjective)			

10. Whose are the gilded tents that crowd the way
    Where all was waste and silent yesterday?

Interrogative pronoun

Gender	masculine	feminine	neuter
Number	singular	plural	
Part of speech	substantive	adjective	adverb
Case (if substantive)	nominative	objective	genitive
Noun modified (if adjective)			

Interrogative pronoun

Gender	masculine	feminine	neuter
Number	singular	plural	
Part of speech	substantive	adjective	adverb
Case (if substantive)	nominative	objective	genitive
Noun modified (if adjective)			

11. Whom did you see at my uncle's?

Interrogative pronoun

Gender	masculine	feminine	neuter
Number	singular	plural	
Part of speech	substantive	adjective	adverb
Case (if substantive)	nominative	objective	genitive
Noun modified (if adjective)			

12. What strange uncertainty is in thy looks?

Interrogative pronoun

Gender	masculine	feminine	neuter
Number	singular	plural	
Part of speech	substantive	adjective	adverb
Case (if substantive)	nominative	objective	genitive
Noun modified (if adjective)			

13. Which of you trembles not that looks on me?

Interrogative pronoun			
Gender	masculine	feminine	neuter
Number	singular	plural	
Part of speech	substantive	adjective	adverb
Case (if substantive)	nominative	objective	genitive
Noun modified (if adjective)			

14. To whom are you speaking?

Interrogative pronoun			
Gender	masculine	feminine	neuter
Number	singular	plural	
Part of speech	substantive	adjective	adverb
Case (if substantive)	nominative	objective	genitive
Noun modified (if adjective)			

15. From whom did you hear this news?

Interrogative pronoun			
Gender	masculine	feminine	neuter
Number	singular	plural	
Part of speech	substantive	adjective	adverb
Case (if substantive)	nominative	objective	genitive
Noun modified (if adjective)			

III.

Write ten exclamatory sentences beginning with *what*.

1. _____

2. _____

3. _____

4. _____

5. _____

6. _____

7. _____

8. _____

9. _____

10. _____

Chapter 126: The Infinitive as a Noun

I.
Replace each infinitive with a verbal noun ending in *-ing* and each noun ending in *-ing* with an infinitive. Thus,

> *To laugh* is peculiar to man.   ------->   *Laughing* is peculiar to man.
> *Fishing* is great sport.   ------->   *To fish* is great sport.

1. To toil is the lot of mankind.

2. To hunt was Roderick's chief delight.

3. To aim and to hit the mark are not the same thing.

4. To swim is easy enough if one has confidence.

5. Wrestling is a favorite rural sport in the South of England.

6. To cross the river was Washington's next task.

7. To be poor is no disgrace.

8. Begging was the poor creature's last resource.

9. Waiting for a train is tedious business.

10. To desert one's flag is disgraceful.

_____

11. Feeling fear is not being a coward.

_____

II.
Analyze the sentences in I, reproduced below, above, as follows:
1. **Underline** the complete subject **once** and the complete predicate **twice**.
2. **Label** the simple subject with **S** and the simple predicate with **V**.
3. **Place** [brackets] around infinitives or verbal nouns and clauses and parentheses around phrases.
4. **Label** direct objects with **DO**, predicate nominatives with **PN**, and predicate adjectives with **PA**.
5. **Label** modifiers (**Adj**, **Adv**, etc.).

1. To toil is the lot of mankind.

2. To hunt was Roderick's chief delight.

3. To aim and to hit the mark are not the same thing.

4. To swim is easy enough if one has confidence.

5. Wrestling is a favorite rural sport in the South of England.

6. To cross the river was Washington's next task.

7. To be poor is no disgrace.

8. Begging was the poor creature's last resource.

9. Waiting for a train is tedious business.

10. To desert one's flag is disgraceful.

11. Feeling fear is not being a coward.

III.

Underline the infinitives and **explain** their construction (e.g. subject, object, etc.). You may wish to review chapter 126, Section 536, as well as the "Extra Resources: Miscellaneous Idioms," Section 7 at the end of this workbook.

1. To save money is sometimes the hardest thing in the world.

_____

2. It is delightful to hear the sound of the sea.

_____

3. It was my wish to join the expedition.

_____

4. Pity it was to hear the elfin's wail.

_____

5. To be faint-hearted is indeed to be unfit for our trade.

_____

6. Her pleasure was to ride the young colts and to scour the plains like Camilla.

_____

7. 'T is thine, O king, the afflicted to redress.

_____

8. The queen's whole design is to act the part of mediator.

_____

Chapter 127: The Infinitive as a Modifier

I.

Underline each infinitive and **label** the construction of each infinitive:

(1) as noun with **N**,

(2) as complementary infinitive (adverbial phrases modifying the verb and completing its sense) with **C**,

(3) as infinitive of purpose (adverbial phrases modifying the verb by adding the purpose of the action) with **P**,

(4) as adjective modifier of a noun (modifies the meaning of a noun and depends upon the noun) with **Adj.**

(5) or as an adverbial modifier of the adjective (modifies the meaning of an adjective and depends upon the adjective) with **Adv.**

The first is done for you.

1. All men strive <u>to excel</u>. **C, completes the sense of** *strive.*

2. I have several times taken up my pen to write to you.

3. The moderate of the other party seem content to have a peace.

4. There was not a moment to be lost.

5. He chanced to enter my office one day.

6. The lawyer had no time to spare.

7. They tried hard to destroy the rats and mice.

8. This was very terrible to see.

9. He continued to advance in spite of every obstacle.

10. Even the birds refused to sing on that sullen day.

11. The bullets began to whistle past them.

12. The fox was quick to see this chance to escape.

13. That gaunt and dusty chamber in Granby Street seemed to smell of seaweed.

14. Resolved to win, he meditates the way.

15. The explorer climbs a peak to survey the country before him.

II.

Make sentences containing each of these words followed by an infinitive:

VERBS:

1. begins _____

_____

2. try _____

_____

3. hoped _____

_____

4. omits _____

_____

5. endeavored _____

_____

6. neglects _____

_____

7. resolved _____

_____

8. strove _____

_____

9. undertook _____

_____

10. determined _____

_____

11. dares _____

_____

12. venture _____

_____

13. desires _____

_____

14. wishes _____

_____

15. longs _____

_____

16. feared _____

_____

ADJECTIVES AND PARTICIPLES:

1. able _____

_____

2. ready _____

_____

3. unwilling _____

_____

4. glad _____

_____

5. loth _____

_____

6. reluctant _____

_____

eager _____

_____

7. sorry _____

_____

8. disposed _____

_____

9. determined _____

_____

10. pleased _____

_____

11. shocked _____

_____

12. gratified _____

_____

13. content _____

_____

14. disturbed _____

_____

Chapter 128: Potential Verb Phrases

I.

Double underline the potential verb phrases. On the line provided, give the meaning of the phrase (see chapter 128 in the text), then **parse** the verb phrases by giving the:

1. tense
2. voice
3. person
4. number

1. She <u>might have held</u> back a little longer. *permitted to have held* _____

past perfect, active voice, third person, singular _____

2. The French officer might as well have said it all aloud. _____

_____

3. Is it possible that you can have talked so wildly? _____

_____

4. An honest man may take a knave's advice. _____

_____

5. If he cannot conquer he may properly retreat. _____

_____

6. I arrived at Oxford with a stock of erudition that might have puzzled a doctor, and a degree

   of ignorance of which a schoolboy would have been ashamed. _____

_____

7. From the hall door she could look down the park. _____

_____

8. Early activity may prevent late and fruitless violence. _____

_____

9. Lear at first could not believe his eyes or ears. _____

_____

10. May I come back to tell you how I succeed? _____

_____

11. We might have had quieter neighbors. _____

_____

12. It must then have been nearly midnight. _____

_____

13. We must have walked at least a mile in this wood. _____

_____

14. When bad men combine, the good must associate. _____

_____

15. I ought to be allowed a reasonable freedom. _____

_____

16. He must and shall come back. _____

_____

17. Something must have happened to Erne._____

_____

18. He would not believe this story, even if you should prove it by trustworthy witnesses._____

_____

_____

19. Would you help me if I should ask it? _____

_____

20. Should you care if I were to fail? _____

_____

21. You should obey me if you were my son._____

_____

22. If he should visit Chicago, would he call on me? _____

_____

23. I would go if the others would. _____

_____

II.
Analyze the sentences in I, which are reproduced below.
1. **Underline** the complete subject **once** and the complete predicate **twice**.
2. **Label** the simple subject with **S** and the simple predicate with **V**.
3. **Place [brackets]** around clauses and **(parentheses)** around phrases.
4. **Label** and identify the parts of phrases (**Prep** and **OP**, etc.).
5. **Label** direct objects with **DO**, predicate nominatives with **PN**, and predicate adjectives with **PA**.
6. **Label** modifiers (**Adj, Adv**, etc.), including phrases.

1. She might have held back a little longer.

2. The French officer might as well have said it all aloud.

3. Is it possible that you can have talked so wildly?

4. An honest man may take a knave's advice.

5. If he cannot conquer he may properly retreat.

6. I arrived at Oxford with a stock of erudition that might have puzzled a doctor, and a degree

   of ignorance of which a schoolboy would have been ashamed.

7. From the hall door she could look down the park.

8. Early activity may prevent late and fruitless violence.

9. Lear at first could not believe his eyes or ears.

10. May I come back to tell you how I succeed?

11. We might have had quieter neighbors.

12. It must then have been nearly midnight.

13. We must have walked at least a mile in this wood.

14. When bad men combine, the good must associate.

15. I ought to be allowed a reasonable freedom.

16. He must and shall come back.

17. Something must have happened to Erne.

18. He would not believe this story, even if you should prove it by trustworthy witnesses.

19. Would you help me if I should ask it?

20. Should you care if I were to fail?

21. You should obey me if you were my son.

22. If he should visit Chicago, would he call on me?

23. I would go if the others would.

Chapter 129: Subjunctive Mood

Written exercises for subjective mood are given in chapter 132.

Chapter 130: Subjunctives in Wishes and Exhortations

Written exercises for subjective mood are given in chapter 132.

Chapter 131: Subjunctive in Concessions, Conditions, Etc.

Written exercises for subjective mood are given in chapter 132.

Chapter 132: Various Uses of the Subjunctive

I.

Make a table of all the indicative and subjunctive forms of the verbs *be, have, do, bind, declare,* in the present and preterite active voice. (See Section 555 or Appendix C and D in your text for help.) Some are done for you.

To Be, Active Voice

INDICATIVE MOOD		SUBJUNCTIVE MOOD	
SINGULAR	PLURAL	SINGULAR	PLURAL
PRESENT TENSE			
1. *I am.* 2. *Thou art.* 3. *He/she/it is.*	_____ _____ _____	1. *If I be.* 2. *If thou be.* 3. *If he/she/it be.*	_____ _____ _____
PRETERITE TENSE			
1. *I was.* 2. _____ 3. _____	_____ _____ _____	1. *If I were.* 2. _____ 3. _____	_____ _____ _____

Have, Active Voice

INDICATIVE MOOD		SUBJUNCTIVE MOOD	
SINGULAR	PLURAL	SINGULAR	PLURAL
PRESENT TENSE			
1. _____ 2. _____ 3. _____	_____ _____ _____	1. _____ 2. _____ 3. _____	_____ _____ _____
PRETERITE TENSE			
1. _____ 2. _____ 3. _____	_____ _____ _____	1. _____ 2. _____ 3. _____	_____ _____ _____

Do, Active Voice

INDICATIVE MOOD		SUBJUNCTIVE MOOD	
SINGULAR	PLURAL	SINGULAR	PLURAL
PRESENT TENSE			
1. _____ 2. _____ 3. _____	_____ _____ _____	1. _____ 2. _____ 3. _____	_____ _____ _____
PRETERITE TENSE			
1. _____ 2. _____ 3. _____	_____ _____ _____	1. _____ 2. _____ 3. _____	_____ _____ _____

Bind, Active Voice

INDICATIVE MOOD		SUBJUNCTIVE MOOD	
SINGULAR	PLURAL	SINGULAR	PLURAL
PRESENT TENSE			
1. _____ 2. _____ 3. _____	_____ _____ _____	1. _____ 2. _____ 3. _____	_____ _____ _____
PRETERITE TENSE			
1. _____ 2. _____ 3. _____	_____ _____ _____	1. _____ 2. _____ 3. _____	_____ _____ _____

Declare, Active Voice

INDICATIVE MOOD		SUBJUNCTIVE MOOD	
SINGULAR	PLURAL	SINGULAR	PLURAL
PRESENT TENSE			
1. _____	_____	1. _____	_____
2. _____	_____	2. _____	_____
3. _____	_____	3. _____	_____
PRETERITE TENSE			
1. _____	_____	1. _____	_____
2. _____	_____	2. _____	_____
3. _____	_____	3. _____	_____

Make a similar table for the present and preterite passive of *send, bind, declare.*

Send, Passive Voice

INDICATIVE MOOD		SUBJUNCTIVE MOOD	
SINGULAR	PLURAL	SINGULAR	PLURAL
PRESENT TENSE			
1. _____	_____	1. _____	_____
2. _____	_____	2. _____	_____
3. _____	_____	3. _____	_____
PRETERITE TENSE			
1. _____	_____	1. _____	_____
2. _____	_____	2. _____	_____
3. _____	_____	3. _____	_____

Bind, Passive Voice

INDICATIVE MOOD		SUBJUNCTIVE MOOD	
SINGULAR	PLURAL	SINGULAR	PLURAL
PRESENT TENSE			
1. _____	_____	1. _____	_____
2. _____	_____	2. _____	_____
3. _____	_____	3. _____	_____
PRETERITE TENSE			
1. _____	_____	1. _____	_____
2. _____	_____	2. _____	_____
3. _____	_____	3. _____	_____

Declare, Passive Voice

INDICATIVE MOOD		SUBJUNCTIVE MOOD	
SINGULAR	PLURAL	SINGULAR	PLURAL
PRESENT TENSE			
1. _____	_____	1. _____	_____
2. _____	_____	2. _____	_____
3. _____	_____	3. _____	_____
PRETERITE TENSE			
1. _____	_____	1. _____	_____
2. _____	_____	2. _____	_____
3. _____	_____	3. _____	_____

II.

Underline the subjunctive in each sentence. **Explain** the form (verb tense and voice), use (e.g. wish, exhortation, supposition, condition, etc.), and meaning of each subjunctive. Refer to chapters 129-132 as you complete this exercise and **write** the Section number from *Mother Tongue II* that applies to that sentence.

1. Mine be a cot beside the hill.

_____

2. Ruin seize thee, ruthless king!

_____

3. It were madness to delay longer.

_____

4. Of great riches there is no real use, except it be in the distribution.

_____

5. King though he be, he may be weak.

_____

6. "God bless you, my dear boy!" Pendennis said to Arthur.

_____

7. It is Jove's doing, and Jove make me thankful!

_____

8. If this were played upon a stage now, I could condemn it as an improbable fiction.

_____

9. Go we, as well as haste will suffer us,

    To this unlooked for, unprepared pomp.

_____

10. If this be treason, make the most of it!

_____

11. "Walk in." "I had rather walk here, I thank you."

_____

12. He looks as if he were afraid.

_____

13. I should have answered if I had been you.

_____

14. God in thy good cause make thee prosperous!

_____

15. These words hereafter thy tormentors be!

_____

16. Had I a son, I would bequeath him a plough.

_____

17. There's matter in't indeed if he be angry.

_____

18. I wish I were at Naples this moment.

_____

19. If he were honest, he would pay his debts.

_____

20. If wishes were horses, beggars might ride.

_____

21. No man cried, "God save him!"

_____

22. By heaven, methinks it were an easy leap

    To pluck bright honor from the pale-faced moon.

---

23. Unless my study and my books be false,

    That argument you held was wrong in you.

---

24. Take heed lest thou fall.

---

25. Though he be angry, he can do no harm.

Chapter 133: The Thought in the Sentence

There are no written exercises for chapter 133.

Chapter 134: Subordinate Clauses Classified

There are no written exercises for chapter 134.

Chapter 135: Clauses of Place and Time

Place **[brackets]** around each subordinate clause that is italicized for you. **Underline** the relative pronoun or relative adverb.

I. ADJECTIVE CLAUSES

1. The town *where John lives* is called Granby.

2. The lion returned to the cave *whence he had come.*

3. Show me the book *in which you found the poem.*

4. There was no water in the desert *through which he passed.*

5. The general fell at the moment *when the enemy began to flee.*

6. Her father died on the day *on which she was born.*

II. ADVERBIAL CLAUSES

1. The soldier died *where he fell.*

2. He found his knife *where he had left it.*

3. You make friends *wherever you are.*

4. *Whither thou goest,* I will go.

5. Washington lived *when George III* was king.

6. The poor fellow works *whenever he can.*

7. We cannot start *while the storm is raging.*

8. Jack rose from bed *as the clock struck six.*

9. We reached our inn *before the sun went down.*

10. Everybody waited *until the speaker had finished.*

11. *When the iron is hot,* then is the time to strike.

Chapter 136: Causal and Concessive Clauses

I.

Make:

1. ten complex sentences containing clauses of time
2. ten containing clauses of place
3. ten containing causal clauses
4. ten containing concessive clauses

Clauses of time

1. _____

2. _____

3. _____

4. _____

5. _____

6. _____

7. _____

8. _____

9. _____

10. _____

Clauses of place

1. _____

2. _____

3. _____

4. _____

5. _____

6. _____

7. _____

8. _____

9. _____

10. _____

Causal clauses

1. _____

2. _____

3. _____

4. _____

5. _____

6. _____

7. _____

8. _____

9. _____

10. _____

Concessive clauses

1. _____

2. _____

3. _____

4. _____

5. _____

6. _____

7. _____

8. _____

9. _____

10. _____

II.

Use each of the following words to introduce a subordinate clause in a complex sentence. For each sentence, tell whether the clause that you have made expresses **time, place, cause,** or **concession.**

1. where _____

_____

2. since _____

_____

3. if _____

_____

4. because_____

_____

5. until _____

_____

6. when_____

_____

7. though _____

_____

Chapter 137: Clauses of Purpose and Result

There are no written exercises for chapter 137.

Chapter 138: Conditional Sentences

There are no written exercises for chapter 138.

Chapter 139: Adverbial Clauses — Comparison

I.
Fill in the blanks below with *he* or **him** as the construction requires.

You are older than _____.

You can run faster than _____.

I am as strong as _____.

We are as careful as _____.

James is a better scholar than _____.

II.
Place [brackets] around each subordinate clause. Tell whether the subordinate clauses express **time, place, cause, concession, condition, purpose, result, or comparison.**

1. As flattery was his trade, he practiced it with the easiest address imaginable. _____

    _____

2. Whenever Macbeth threatened to do mischief to anyone, he was sure to keep his word.

    _____

3. His armor was so good that he had no fear of arrows._____

    _____

4. We admire his bravery, though it is shown in a bad cause._____

    _____

5. He talks as if he were a Spaniard. _____

6. The marble bridge is the resort of everybody, where they hear music, eat iced fruits, and

    sup by moonlight. _____

7. It was a fortnight after this, before the two brothers met again._____

    _____

8. It was impossible for me to climb this stile, because every step was six feet high. _____

    _____

9. The troops were hastily collected, that an assault might be made without delay. _____

_____

10. Let us therefore stop while to stop is in our power. _____

11. King Robert was silent when he heard this story. _____

12. If others have blundered, it is your place to put them to right. _____

13. If Milton had any virtues, they are not to be found in the Doctor's picture of him.

_____

14. Where foams and flows the glorious Rhine,

    Many a ruin wan and gray

O'erlooks the cornfield and the vine,

    Majestic in its dark decay.

_____

15. It was impossible for me to advance a step; for the stalks were so interwoven that I could

not creep through. _____

16. If he is not here by Saturday, I shall go after him. _____

17. He laid his ear to the ground that he might hear their steps. _____

18. My passage by sea from Rotterdam to England was more painful to me than all the

journeys I had ever made by land. _____

19. Weeds were sure to grow quicker in his fields than anywhere else. _____

_____

Chapter 140: Direct and Indirect Statements

I.

Change the following statements to the form of **indirect quotation** after "He said that." The first one is done for you.

> EXAMPLE: "I found this diamond in South Africa."
> He said that he found that diamond in South Africa.

1. I found this diamond in South Africa. _____

_____

2. I shall sail for Yokohama next Tuesday. _____

_____

3. My grandfather has given me a gold watch. _____

_____

4. I am not fond of poetry. _____

_____

5. I honor the memory of Mr. Gladstone. _____

_____

6. Lieutenant Peary has just returned from the Arctic regions._____

_____

7. You will certainly visit the pyramids. _____

_____

8. John is stronger than Thomas. _____

_____

9. This bird's wing has been broken. _____

_____

10. The trapper is struggling with a huge bear. _____

_____

11. My home is on the prairie. _____

_____

12. Louisiana formerly belonged to France. _____

_____

II.

Turn each sentence from Exercise I into a direct quotation using quotation marks and the prefix "He said," and compare the results with the original sentences. Be sure to punctuate properly.

1. I found this diamond in South Africa. _____

_____

2. I shall sail for Yokohama next Tuesday. _____

_____

3. My grandfather has given me a gold watch. _____

_____

4. I am not fond of poetry. _____

_____

5. I honor the memory of Mr. Gladstone. _____

_____

6. Lieutenant Peary has just returned from the Arctic regions. _____

_____

7. You will certainly visit the pyramids. _____

_____

8. John is stronger than Thomas. _____

_____

9. This bird's wing has been broken. _____

_____

10. The trapper is struggling with a huge bear. _____

_____

11. My home is on the prairie. _____

_____

12. Louisiana formerly belonged to France. _____

_____

Chapter 141: Indirect Questions

Place **[brackets]** around the substantive clauses. **Label** the construction of each (as subject with **Sub**, object with **Obj**, predicate nominative with **PN**), and **write** in the blank on the left whether it is an indirect statement (**S**) or an indirect question (**Q**). The first is done for you.

1. <u>**Sub, S**</u>   [That fine feathers do not make fine birds] has always been taught by philosophers.

2. _____Here we halted in the open field, and sent out our people to see how things were in the country.

3. _____I do not imagine that you find me rash in declaring myself.

4. _____What became of my companions I cannot tell.

5. _____I should now tell what public measures were taken by the magistrates for the general safety.

6. _____You see, my lord, how things are altered.

7. _____Now the question was, what I should do next.

8. _____He said that he was going over to Greenwich. I asked if he would let me go with him.

9. _____That the tide is rising may be seen by anybody.

10. _____Ask me no reason why I love you.

11. _____That Arnold was a traitor was now clear enough.

12. _____I doubt whether this act is legal.

13. _____I am not prepared to say that Knox had a soft temper; nor do I know that he had an ill temper.

14. _____There are two questions, — whether the Essay will succeed, and who or what is the author.

15. _____The shouts of storm and successful violence announced that the castle was in the

act of being taken.

16. _____The stranger inquired where the mayor lived.

17. _____That all is not gold that glitters was found out long ago.

18. _____I demanded why the gates were shut.

19. _____I doubt if I ever talked so much nonsense in my life.

20. _____I solemnly assure you that you are quite mistaken.

21. _____The prince soon concluded that he should never be happy in this course of life.

22. _____I know not what others may think.

23. _____Tell me not that life is a dream.

24. _____I think you are mistaken.

Chapter 142: Infinitive Clauses

Make ten sentences containing infinitive clauses after verbs of *wishing, commanding, believing, declaring,* etc. Here are some examples:

Joanna told her to sing a song. (Verb of *commanding*)

Hope declares him to be the winner. (Verb of *declaring*)

1. _____

_____

2. _____

_____

3. _____

_____

4. _____

_____

5. _____

_____

6. _____

_____

7. _____

_____

8. _____

_____

9. _____

_____

10. _____

_____

Chapter 143: Elliptical Sentences

Rewrite and **supply** the ellipsis in each of the following elliptical sentences. Study the examples in chapter 143 to help you.

1. When in need of help, apply to me.

_____

2. The leader they chose was called Pedro.

_____

3. A good conscience is better than gold.

_____

4. You are much taller than I.

_____

5. Tom likes you better than me.

_____

6. Though beaten, I am not discouraged.

_____

7. I will send you the money tomorrow, if possible.

_____

8. Why all this noise?

_____

9. Some of us are studying arithmetic, others algebra.

_____

10. The book you were reading has been returned to the library.

_____

11. I don't believe you know your lesson.

_____

12. What next?

_____

13. When inclined to lose your temper, count twenty before you speak.

_____

14. "Whither bound?" asked the captain.

_____

15. Beetles have six legs, spiders eight.

_____

16. Your boat is painted white, George's green.

_____

17. I bought this hat at Sampson's.

_____

18. These apples, though handsome enough, are rather hard.

_____

Punctuation Practice: Exercise A

Copy the following sentences and make all capitalization and punctuation corrections.

1. is it your will brethren that this man be elected to the council

_____

_____

2. hark how the pitiless tempest raves

_____

3. tom however was not pleased with the prospect

_____

_____

4. nothing i trust will interfere with your plan

_____

5. the fisherman wades in the surges

_____

   the sailor sails over the sea

_____

   the soldier steps bravely to battle

_____

   the woodman lays axe to the tree

_____

6. neither witch nor warlock crossed mordaunt's path however

_____

_____

Punctuation Practice: Exercise B

Copy the following sentences and make all capitalization and punctuation corrections.

1. the horse was injured in one of his hind legs.

    _____

    _____

2. esther was going to see if she could get some fresh eggs for her mistresss breakfast before the shops closed.

    _____

    _____

3. all speech even the commonest speech has something of song in it

    _____

    _____

4. sam ran out to hold his Fathers horse

    _____

    _____

5. now doctor cried the boys do tell us your adventures

    _____

    _____

6. our english archers bent their bows

   their hearts were good and true

   at the first flight of arrows sent

   full fourscore scots they slew

   _____

   _____

   _____

   _____

7. the bridegroom stood dangling his bonnet and plume

   _____

   _____

8. emma was sitting in the midst of the children telling them a story and she came smiling

   towards Erne holding out her hand

   _____

   _____

Punctuation Practice: Exercise C[5]

Copy the following opening sentence from Charles Dickens's *Tale of Two Cities*, adding commas where they belong. Dickens uses a series of parallel clauses to give the setting for his book. He chose to use commas rather than semicolons, which are sometime used to set off independent clauses. The dash after "way" is provided for you.

Hint: There are 17 commas missing.

It was the best of times it was the worst of times it was the age of wisdom it was the age of foolishness it was the epoch of belief it was the epoch of incredulity it was the season of light it was the season of darkness it was the spring of hope it was the winter of despair we had everything before us we had nothing before us we were all going direct to Heaven we were all going direct the other way--in short the period was so far like the present period that some of its noisiest authorities insisted on its being received for good or for evil in the superlative degree of comparison only.

_____

_____

_____

_____

_____

_____

_____

_____

_____

_____

_____

_____

---

[5] Note: This exercise is provided as a supplement. It did not appear in the original *Mother Tongue Book II*.

Punctuation Practice: Exercise D[6]

Copy the following dialogue from Jane Austen's *Pride and Prejudice* and make all capitalization and punctuation corrections, adding quotation marks as needed.

Hint: The paragraphing is done correctly, which gives you an indication of the change in speaker. Some periods and commas are given, which are correct. There are six missing commas, two missing semicolons, two missing question marks, two missing periods, and five missing pairs of quotation marks.

do you talk by rule then while you are dancing

sometimes. one must speak a little you know. it would look odd to be entirely silent for half an hour together and yet for the advantage of *some* conversation ought to be so arranged as that they may have the trouble of saying as little as possible

are you consulting your own feelings in the present case, or do you imagine that you are gratifying mine

both replied elizabeth archly for I have always seen a great similarity in the turn of our minds

_____

_____

_____

_____

_____

_____

_____

_____

_____

_____

_____

_____

---

[6] Note: This exercise is provided as a supplement. It did not appear in the original *Mother Tongue Book II*.

Punctuation Practice: Exercise E[7]

Copy the following excerpted dialogue, which is taken from Anna Sewell's *Black Beauty*, adding proper punctuation and capitals.

Hint: In the selection below there are four missing capital letters, two missing pairs of quotation marks, one pair of single quotation marks, four missing commas, one missing hyphen, one missing period, and one missing question mark.

yes she said; he is really quite a beauty and he has such a sweet good

tempered face and such a fine intelligent eye what do you say to calling him black

beauty?

_____

_____

_____

_____

_____

Hint: In the selection below there are five missing capitals, one missing pair of quotation marks, three missing commas, and three missing periods. The dash is provided for you.

black beauty--why yes i think that is a very good name if you like it shall be

his name and so it was

_____

_____

_____

---

[7] Note: This exercise is provided as a supplement. It did not appear in the original *Mother Tongue Book II*.

Hint: In the selection below there are seven missing capitals, five missing commas, and one missing period.

when john went into the stable he told james that master and mistress had chosen a good sensible english name for me that meant something; not like marengo or pegasus or abdallah

_____

_____

_____

Why do you think there is a semicolon placed after *something*? _____

_____

Hint: In the selection below there are seven missing capitals, three missing commas, one missing pair of quotation marks, and one missing period.

they both laughed; and james said if it was not for bringing back the past i should have named him rob roy for i never saw two horses more alike

_____

_____

_____

_____

Punctuation Practice: Exercise F[8]

Copy the following selection, which is taken from Mark Twain's *The Celebrated Jumping Frog of Calaberas County,* and provide the missing punctuation. In it, Mark Twain uses commas to set off clauses and uses a semicolon to divide the sentence at the point of the conjunction.

Hint: There are seven commas missing and one semicolon missing.

He never smiled he never frowned he never changed his voice from the gentle-flowing key to which he tuned the initial sentence he never betrayed the slightest suspicion of enthusiasm but all through the interminable narrative there ran a vein of impressive earnestness and sincerity which showed me plainly that so far from his imagining that there was anything ridiculous or funny about his story he regarded it as a really important matter and admired its two heroes as men of transcendent genius in *finesse.*

---

[8] Note: This exercise is provided as a supplement. It did not appear in the original *Mother Tongue Book II.*

Final Review: Exercise A

Analyze the following sentences by labeling the subject, verb, objects and modifiers. Be sure to mark clauses with brackets and phrases with parentheses and identify their function in the sentence (adverbial, adjective, object, etc.).[9] You do not need to label the parts of each prepositional phrase.

Write answers to the thinking questions about each sentence, or discuss orally with your teacher.

1. They have lighted the islands with ruin's torch.

   a. What is the verb tense and voice of *have lighted*? _____

   b. What kind of phrase is *with ruin's torch*? _____

   c. What does it modify? _____

2. A row of tall Lombardy poplars guarded the western side of the old mansion.

   a. What is the verb tense and voice of *guarded*? _____

   b. Rewrite the sentence with all modifying words and phrases **removed** (except articles):

   _____

   c. Change the sentence by adding in your own modifiers. _____

   _____

   d. Did you change the meaning of the sentence entirely? _____

3. The geologist says that a glacier resembles a river in many respects.

   a. Is this a direct or indirect statement? _____

   b. Explain the function of *that* in this sentence (see chapter 140). _____

---

[9] Final review sentences are taken from *The Mother Tongue Book II Revised Edition*, © 1908. The additional questions about each sentence have been added by the editors.

4. Though many years have elapsed since I trod the drowsy shades of Sleepy Hollow, I question whether I should not still find the same trees and the same families vegetating in its sheltered bosom.

   a. What is the potential verb phrase in this complex sentence? _____

   b. *Though many years have elapsed since I trod the drowsy shades of Sleepy Hollow* is classified as what kind of clause? (See chapter 136.) _____

   c. Sometimes sentences beginning with this sort of clause are in the subjunctive mood (see chapters 129-132). Do you think this sentence is in the subjunctive?_____

   d. Why or why not? _____

5. I think that I have not yet told you how we left that charming place, Genoa.

   a. What is the appositive in this sentence and what noun does it modify? _____

   b. How is the phrase *that charming place, Genoa* functioning in the sentence?_____

   c. How is the clause *how we left that charming place, Genoa* functioning in the sentence?

   _____

6. The rain swept down from the half-seen hills, wreathed the wooded peaks with a gray garment of mist, and filled the valley with a whitish cloud.

   a. Is this a simple, compound, or complex sentence? _____

   b. There are three verbs. List them and tell if they are transitive or intransitive._____

   _____

   c. Why is *down* an adverb and not a preposition in this instance? _____

7. If the whole world should agree that *yes* and *no* should change their meanings, *yes* would deny, and *no* would affirm.

    a. This sentence begins with *If*. What are these kinds of sentences called?_____

    _____

    b. Write the main clause here:_____

    c. What is the sentence's mood? _____

8. One of the company remarked that prudence should be distinguished from fear.

    a. What is the simple subject and predicate of the main clause? _____

    b. What is the simple subject and predicate of the subordinate clause? _____

    _____

    c. What is the mood of the subordinate clause's verb phrase? _____

9. The dry basin of a fountain, and a few trees, ragged and unpruned, indicate that this spot, in past days, was a pleasant, shady retreat, filled with fruits and flowers and a sweet murmur of waters.

    a. How does chapter 101, section 428 describe a participle? _____

    _____

    b. Write the participle phrase that describes *retreat*. _____

    c. What clause functions as the direct object of *indicate*? _____

    _____

    _____

10. An ancient writer reports that the sum of Persian education consisted in teaching the youth to ride, to shoot with the bow, and to speak the truth.

   a. List the infinitives. _____

   b. Write the preposition phrase that begins with the preposition *in* and label its parts.

   _____

   _____

   c. Write the phrase that is the object of the preposition *in.* _____

   _____

   d. The participle *teaching* takes three objects. What are the three object phrases? _____

   _____

   e. What is the function of *the youth* in this sentence? _____

   f. Which infinitive takes an object? What is the object of this infinitive? _____

   _____

Final Review: Exercise B

Analyze the following sentences by labeling the subject, verb, objects and modifiers. Be sure to mark clauses with brackets and phrases with parentheses and identify their function in the sentence (adverbial, adjective, object, etc.).[10] You do not need to label the parts of each prepositional phrase.

Write answers to the thinking questions about each sentence, or discuss orally with your teacher.

1. Those who in their lives were applauded and admired, are sometimes laid at last in the

   ground without the common honor of a stone.

   a. What is the simple subject and predicate of this sentence? _____

   _____

   b. Write the relative clause that modifies the pronoun *Those*. _____

   _____

   c. Is it restrictive or descriptive? _____

2. Betrayed, deserted, disorganized, unprovided with resources, begirt with enemies, the

   whole city was still no easy conquest.

   a. List the participles._____

   _____

   b. What substantive do the participles modify adjectively? _____

---

[10] Final review sentences are taken from *The Mother Tongue Book II Revised Edition*, © 1908. The additional questions about each sentence have been added by the editors.

3. The progress of agriculture has led to the draining of mosses, the felling of forests, and the transformation of heaths and wastes into arable land.

    a. What is the simple subject and predicate of this sentence? _____

    b. Is this a simple, compound, or complex sentence? _____

    c. Are the words *draining* and *felling* participles or verbal nouns (gerunds)? Why? _____

    _____

    d. The preposition *to* has multiple objects. What are they? _____

    _____

    e. List the prepositional phrases. _____

    _____

4. The autumn wind wandered among the branches. It whirled away the leaves from all except the pine-trees, and moaned as if it lamented the desolation which it caused.

    a. Write the simple subject and predicate of both sentences._____

    b. Is the second sentence a simple, compound, or complex sentence? _____

    c. Write the simple subject and predicate of the subordinate clause that modifies *moaned*.

    _____

    d. Write the subordinate clause that modifies *desolation*. _____

5. Beneath the shelter of one hut, in the bright blaze of the same fire, sat this varied group of adventurers.

   a. Write the simple subject and predicate. _____

   b. Why do you think the author inverted the order of this sentence, placing the predicate first? _____

   c. Write a sentence in the same pattern, with the same subject and verb, but create your own adverbial and adjective phrases. Here is the pattern:

      (Adverbial phrase with adjective phrase)-(Adverbial phrase with adjective phrase)-(**sat**)-(Adjective-Adjective-**group**)-(Adjective phrase) _____

      _____

      _____

6. One gains nothing by attempting to shut out the sprites of the weather. They come in at the keyhole; they peer through the dripping panes; they insinuate themselves through the crevices of the casement, or plump themselves down the chimney astride of the raindrops.

   a. Write the simple subject, predicate and object of the first sentence._____

   _____

   b. The second sentence is compound. List the pairs of subjects and verbs for each independent clause. _____

   _____

   c. List any participles, infinitives, and verbal nouns and write their part of speech in the sentences (e.g. adjective, object, etc.)_____

   _____

   _____

7. Miss Jessie Brown was ten years younger than her sister, and twenty shades prettier.

    a. Write the adjectives of comparison._____

    b. Are they the comparative or superlative degree? _____

    c. This sentence is an elliptical sentence (see chapter 143). What are the missing words and

    where should they go? _____

8. How few appear in those streets which but some few hours ago were crowded!

    a. The subordinate clause begins with the relative pronoun *which*. What is its antecedent?

    _____

    b. Can you tell what kind of phrase *but some few hours ago* is? _____

    c. The word *few* appears twice in this sentence. What is the part of speech of *few* in each

    instance? _____

9. From these quiet windows the figures of passing travelers looked too remote and dim to

    disturb the sense of privacy.

    a. Write the simple subject and predicate._____

    b. What is the function of the infinitive phrase *to disturb the sense of privacy*? _____

    _____

    c. Does the infinitive *to disturb* take an object? If so, what is it?_____

10. There is exquisite delight in picking up for one's self an arrowhead that was dropped

centuries ago and has never been handled since.

   a. What is the subject of this sentence? _____

   b. Read the "Extra Resources: Miscellaneous Idioms" chapter in this workbook. Explain

      why *there* is not the subject and tell what *there* is called when used in this way. _____

_____

   c. What is the other pronoun that is often used in English as a filler, just as *there*? _____

   d. Is the demonstrative *that* used substantively as a pronoun or as an adjective in this

      sentence? _____

Final Review: Exercise C

Analyze the following sentences by labeling the subject, verb, objects and modifiers. Be sure to mark clauses with brackets and phrases with parentheses and identify their function in the sentence (adverbial, adjective, object, etc.).[11] You do not need to label the parts of each prepositional phrase.

Write answers to the thinking questions about each sentence, or discuss orally with your teacher.

1. Sea air ripens friendship quicker than the hotbed of a city.

    a. What two groups of words are connected by the conjunction *than*? _____

    _____

    b. What two settings are being compared in this sentence? _____

    c. Write your own sentence telling what you think "...ripens friendship quicker than..."

    _____

    _____

2. The weather was so bad that I could not embark that night.

    a. The demonstrative *that* is used twice in this sentence. How is each one used? As a

    conjunction? Substantively as a pronoun? Or adjectively? Give your reasons. _____

    _____

    b. Refer to chapters 134-137 and classify the subordinate clause._____

---

[11] Final review sentences are taken from *The Mother Tongue Book II Revised Edition*, © 1908. The additional questions about each sentence have been added by the editors.

3. Amsterdam was the place where the leading Scotch and English assembled.

    a. List the proper nouns. _____

    b. Rewrite this as a simple sentence without losing any meaning._____

    _____

4. He shouts as if he were trying his voice against a northwest gale of wind.

    a. Write the main clause. _____

    b. Is the subordinate clause an adverbial or adjective clause? _____

    c. What is the verb tense and number of *shouts?*_____

    d. What is the verb tense and number of *were trying?*_____

    e. What is the mood of the main clause? _____

    f. What is the mood of the subordinate clause? _____

5. Captain Brown and Miss Jenkyns were not very cordial to each other.

    a. What kind of pronoun is *each other*? _____

    b. Is it a substantive or adjective in this sentence? _____

6. For a moment his life was in jeopardy.

    a. Parse the pronoun *his,* giving the gender, number, and case. _____

    b. Write the phrases and tell what their part of speech in the sentence is. _____

    _____

7. Martha was blunt and plain-spoken to a fault.

   a. Why is *plain-spoken* hyphenated?_____

   b. What kind of verb is *was* in this sentence? _____

8. The old man had become sluggish and self-indulgent.

   a. Write the simple subject and predicate. _____

   b. Parse the verb phrase and give its tense, person, and number. _____

   c. Is the verb phrase transitive or intransitive? _____

9. The major had a wiry, well-trained, elastic figure, a stiff military throw-back of his head,

   and a springing step.

   a. Parse the verb phrase and give its tense, person, and number. _____

   b. Is the verb phrase transitive or intransitive? _____

   c. List the three direct objects. _____

10. The traveler quickened his pace when he reached the outskirts of the town, for a gloomy

    extent of nearly four miles lay between him and his home.

    a. There are four pronouns in this sentence. Parse them by giving their gender, number,

       and case._____

       1) _____

2) _____

3) _____

4) _____

b. Is this a compound, complex, or compound-complex sentence? Why? _____

_____

Final Review: Exercise D

Analyze the following sentences by labeling the subject, verb, objects and modifiers. Be sure to mark clauses with brackets and phrases with parentheses and identify their function in the sentence (adverbial, adjective, object, etc.).[12] You do not need to label the parts of each prepositional phrase.

Write answers to the thinking questions about each sentence, or discuss orally with your teacher.

1. The conversation of the passengers in the coach was gay and animated.

    a. Rewrite the sentence, replacing the *of*-phrase with the genitive and keeping the meaning

    intact. _____

    _____

    b. Rewrite the sentence, but this time make *passengers* the subject and use *conversed* as the

    verb. What must you do to *gay* and *animated*?_____

    _____

2. The silver light, with quivering glance,

    Played on the water's expanse.

    a. What is the simple subject and simple predicate? _____

    b. Write a new sentence, following the same pattern, but use *"Leaves rustled"* as the simple

    subject and predicate. _____

    _____

---

[12] Final review sentences are taken from *The Mother Tongue Book II Revised Edition*, © 1908. The additional questions about each sentence have been added by the editors.

c. Write a new sentence, following the same pattern, but use *"Sound echoed"* as the simple

subject and predicate. _____

_____

3. The appearance of Rip, with his long grizzled beard, his rusty fowling piece, his uncouth

dress, and the army of women and children that had gathered at his heels, soon attracted

the attention of the tavern politicians.

a. What is the simple subject and simple predicate? _____

b. What are the objects of the preposition *with*? _____

4. Nature never hurries. Atom by atom, little by little, she achieves her work.

a. What word do you think the idiomatic phrases *Atom by atom* and *little by little* modify?

_____

b. Parse the pronouns *she* and *her*, giving their gender, number, and case._____

_____

c. What is the antecedent? _____

d. What kind of noun (common or proper, abstract or concrete) is *Nature*? _____

5. The sky was clear, and a single star shown out sharply.

   a. Is this sentence compound, complex, or compound-complex? Why?_____

   b. Parse the verbs and give their tense, number, and tell if they are transitive or

   intransitive? _____

   _____

6. Fast are the flying moments, faster are the hoofs of our horses.

   a. What are the degrees of comparison for the adjectives? _____

   b. Identify the words used in alliteration._____

7. We trod the fire out, locked the door, and set forth upon our walk.

   a. List the simple subject and simple predicates._____

   b. Parse the verbs and give their tense, voice (active or passive), person, and number. _____

   _____

8. No man's power can be equal to his will.

   a. What kind of verb phrase is *can be*?_____

   b. What is the past form of *can*? _____

   c. What is the meaning of *can* and *may*? _____

9. Everything which helps a boy's power of observation, helps his power of learning.

    a. List the substantives and identify their case (nominative, genitive, objective). _____

    _____

    b. Is *which* a descriptive or restrictive relative pronoun (see chapter 121)? _____

10. While many a thoughtless person is whirled through Europe without gaining a single idea,

    the observing eye and inquiring mind find matter of improvement and delight in every

    ramble.

    a. Write the participles and explain their function in the sentence. _____

    _____

    b. Refer to chapters 134-139 and identify the category of the subordinate clause in this

    sentence. _____

Final Review: Exercise E

Analyze the following sentences by labeling the subject, verb, objects and modifiers. Be sure to mark clauses with brackets and phrases with parentheses and identify their function in the sentence (adverbial, adjective, object, etc.).[13] You do not need to label the parts of each prepositional phrase.

Write answers to the thinking questions about each sentence, or discuss orally with your teacher.

1. Sweet smiling village, loveliest of the lawn,

    Thy sports are fled, and all thy charms withdrawn.

    a. What is the phrase "sweet smiling village, loveliest of the lawn," called in this sentence?

    _____

    b. How should it be treated in analysis? _____

2. The bristling burdock, the sweet-scented catnip, and the humble yarrow planted

    themselves along the woodland road.

    a. What is the self-pronoun in this sentence?_____

    b. Is it an intensive pronoun or an object? _____

3. Be just and fear not.

    a. Is this a declarative, imperative, or interrogative sentence? _____

    b. What is the second person indicative form of the verb *to be*? _____

---

[13] Final review sentences are taken from *The Mother Tongue Book II Revised Edition,* © 1908. The additional questions about each sentence have been added by the editors.

c. Why is it *be* in this sentence? _____

4. Fear makes man a slave to others.

   a. Is *fear* an abstract or concrete noun? _____

   b. Refer to chapter 118. Why is *slave* a predicate objective (also called complementary

   object)? _____

5. He who plants a tree plants a hope.

   a. Write the main clause. _____

   b. Write the subordinate clause. _____

   c. What is the relative pronoun? _____What is its function in the

   clause? _____

6. The birds were hopping and twittering among the bushes, and the eagle was wheeling aloft

   and breasting the pure mountain breeze.

   a. Write the verbs and parse them, giving their tense and voice, person, and number.

   _____

7. I threw aside the newspaper, and explored my way to the kitchen, to take a peep at the

   group that seemed so merry.

   a. Rewrite this sentence replacing all the verbs. _____

   _____

   _____

   b. Write the simple subject and predicate. _____

8. You think me, no doubt, a tardy correspondent.

   a. Parse each pronoun and give its gender, number, and case. _____

   b. Why is *correspondent* a predicate objective? Refer to chapter 118._____

   _____

9. The fugitives broke down the bridges and burned the ferryboats.

   a. Is *down* an adverb or preposition?_____

   b. Is this a simple sentence with a compound predicate or a complex sentence? _____

   _____

10. Somebody tapped me on the shoulder, and I saw a couple of rough-looking fellows behind

me.

    a. Is this a compound or complex sentence? _____

    b. List the pronouns and give their gender, number, and case._____

_____

Final Review: Exercise F

Analyze the following sentences by labeling the subject, verb, objects and modifiers. Be sure to mark clauses with brackets and phrases with parentheses and identify their function in the sentence (adverbial, adjective, object, etc.).[14] You do not need to label the parts of each prepositional phrase.

Write answers to the thinking questions about each sentence, or discuss orally with your teacher.

1. The courtyard was in an uproar, the house in a bustle. _____

    a. Is this a simple, compound, or complex sentence? _____

    b. What is the verb for the subject *house*? _____

    c. What are sentences like this one called? _____

    d. Review the list of sentences in chapter 143, Section 620. Write the sentence that matches

        this pattern. _____

        _____

2. He seldom, it is true, sent his eyes or his thoughts beyond the boundaries of his own farm;

    but within those boundaries everything was snug, happy, and well-conditioned.

    a. Why is this sentence divided with a semi-colon? _____

    b. Is this a compound, complex, or compound-complex sentence? Why? _____

    _____

---

[14] Final review sentences are taken from *The Mother Tongue Book II Revised Edition*, © 1908. The additional questions about each sentence have been added by the editors.

3. With rushing winds and gloomy skies

   The dark and stubborn winter dies.

   a. Rewrite this couplet with the complete subject first and the complete predicate second.

   _____

   _____

   b. Why do you think the poet chose to divide the predicate? _____

   _____

4. How many of the enemy were taken he did not know.

   a. Parse *were taken* and give its tense, number, and person._____

   b. What is the subject and its number? _____

   c. Why isn't this sentence punctuated with a question mark? _____

5. I loved the brimming wave that swam

   Through quiet meadows round the mill.

   a. What kind of clause is the subordinate clause?_____

   b. Is the demonstrative *that* used as a conjunction, substantively as a pronoun, or as an

      adjective? _____

6. The crows were wheeling behind the plough in scattering clusters.

    a. Write the simple subject and predicate. _____

    b. Parse the verb phrase by giving its tense, person, and number._____

    c. Write the participles and tell the function of each one in the sentence._____

    _____

7. History informs us that Louisiana once belonged to France.

    a. Which nouns are proper nouns? _____

    b. Which noun is an abstract noun?_____

    c. What is the function of the subordinate clause in the sentence? _____

Extra Resources: Miscellaneous Idioms[15]

1. A number of **idioms** which often give rise to doubt and discussion are here brought together for reference.

2. The **possessive** is often used, especially in the predicate, without a noun.

> This horse is my *uncle's* [horse].
> I bought this coat at *Johnson's*.
> That book is *mine* [=my book].

3. The **possessive** without a noun may be used after *of*.

> I am a friend *of Tom's*. [=I am one of Tom's friends.]
> A neighbor *of mine* shot a hawk yesterday. [=One of my neighbors.]

The phrase "a friend *of Tom's*" is equivalent to "a friend of (=*from among*) Tom's friends," that is, "one of Tom's friends."

4. The possessive is regularly used before the verbal noun ending in *-ing*.

> I was sure of *its* being he. [Not: *it*.]
> I had heard of *John's* winning the prize. [Not: *John*.]

5. The **article** or the possessive should be repeated with two or more connected nouns or adjectives whenever clearness or precision requires it. Thus,

> I will confer with *the* secretary and *the* treasurer.

In such sentences as the following, no repetition is necessary, since no confusion is possible:

> I will ask all *the boys and girls* in my class.
> He was very fond of *his father and mother*.[16]

In doubtful cases, however, it is safer to repeat.

---

[15] From *Mother Tongue Book II Revised, c. 1908. These sections appears as sections 611-620.*

[16] Hard and fast rules calling for repetition in sentences like these are common in textbooks but are not justified by good usage. [Original footnote from Kittredge and Arnold.]

6. The **adverb** *there* may be used merely to introduce a sentence without expressing any idea of place.

> There is a famine.
> There are spots in the sun.
> There came a change over the landscape.

This is sometimes called the **expletive** use of *there.*

7. The pronoun *it* may serve merely to introduce the copula *is* in a sentence. in this use the pronoun *it* is often called an **expletive**.

> It is I.
> It was a great pity
> It is wise to be watchful.

In such sentences, *it* is the grammatical subject. The real subject of the thought, however, appears in the predicate.

Thus, in the first example, the subject of the thought (*I*) appears as a predicate nominative; in the third, the phrase *to be watchful* (the real subject of the thought) may be regarded as grammatically in apposition with *it* (see chapter 126, section 536 in *The Mother Tongue: Adapted for Modern Students*).

8. A verb of *asking* may take two objects, one denoting the **person** and the other thing **thing**. The second of these may be retained after the passive.

> I asked the *lawyer* his *opinion.*
> The lawyer was asked his *opinion.*

Note: Similarly, such a sentence as "They gave John permission" may become, in the passive, "John was given permission." It is neater, however, to write "John received permission."

9. Besides the article *the*, there is an **adverb** *the*, which is used with comparatives to express the **degree of difference.**

> When the task is difficult, we should try *the* harder.
> He ran all *the* more rapidly when we called upon him to halt.
> The more a man has, *the* more he wants.

In the third example, the first *the* is relative and the second demonstrative in sense, "*By how much* a man as more, *by so much* he wants more."

10. The **present tense** often has a **future** meaning.

   The steamer *sails* on Friday.
   Tomorrow is Saturday.
   If I *see* John tomorrow, I will give him your message.

Made in United States
North Haven, CT
09 August 2023

40119565R00124